CHARLES E. MADDRY

AN AUTOBIOGRAPHY

Charles E. Maddry

An Autobiography

Broadman Press

NASHVILLE • TENNESSEE

Printed in the United States of America
1.5 O 54 R.R.D.

Foreword

AFTER TEN YEARS the undertaking has been completed. The work of writing this manuscript has been done in the midst of a busy and crowded life. Many have helped me along the way or I never could have finished the task.

First, I want to acknowledge with deep gratitude the help and inspiration received from my classmate and long-time professor of creative writing in the University of North Carolina, Charles Phillips Russell. At the age of seventy-one years, I re-entered the University and studied for several months under this popular and inspiring teacher. Several of the chapters of this book were read before his classes and received the constructive criticism of my teacher and classmates.

I would also pay grateful tribute to Miss Lucile Rogers, professor in the department of English of Union University, Jackson, Tennessee. She has had wide experience in the making of books and in editorial work.

I would also acknowledge with sincere appreciation the valuable assistance of Miss Linda Maddry, a secretary in the department of mathematics at State College, Raleigh, North Carolina. She is a splendid stenographer and has copied and re-copied the manuscript many times. Without her assistance, I could not have finished the undertaking.

Dr. E. C. Routh of Lockhart, Texas, former editor of *The Commission* of the Baptist Foreign Mission Board, edited the manuscript and checked many of the historical references in the book.

I would also pay glad tribute to Dr. Hight C Moore, former editorial secretary of the Sunday School Board, for many valuable suggestions made while the manuscript was in preparation.

I wish also to express my great appreciation to my wife for her encouragement through the years. Many times the work was laid aside during the press of other duties but, always under her sympathetic inspiration, was taken up afresh.

And lastly, to my granddaughter, Kay Maddry Severance, now

a student at Westhampton College, Richmond, I would acknowledge valuable assistance rendered in searching out and correcting mistakes in spelling, choice of words, and construction.

So to all these fellow helpers along the way, I express my deep and sincere gratitude.

I pray earnestly that God's blessing may be upon all who by chance may read the story of my experiences as I have traveled the pathways of the world.

CHARLES E. MADDRY

Hillsboro, North Carolina

Contents

List of Illustrations

Introduction

I

Here is the very radiant record of a boy who rose from rural obscurity to worldwide influence.

He came of sturdy stock with high forehead to think, keen eyes to see, firm jaws to will, throbbing heart to feel, strong hands to work, swift feet to run the race of life.

He was brought up in exhilarant environs: on a fertile farm of primitive equipment; in a home of good parents and happy children; among friendly neighbors; in a region of high uplook and far outlook.

Through seemingly limited circumstances, he was given large insight from the home hearth, the church services, the public schools, a modest supply of good literature, and occasional addresses of ability.

From divine fingerboards he was guided in every step of his preparatory years—from his conversion and baptism and call to the ministry to his ordination and student pastorates until he graduated with honor from the state university near his home and from theological seminary at Louisville.

He was most fortunate in winning for his life-partner "a worthy woman," and their beautifully blended lives were radiantly happy and widely blest for nearly fifty years, their gifted daughter with her husband and children rising up "to call them blessed."

He was a popular pastor of grateful and growing churches: "a good minister of Jesus Christ;" effective in evangelism, energetic in upbuilding and outreaching; eminent in pulpit power; outstanding in his denomination; an esteemed citizen of the commonwealth and the kingdom.

He was an administrator of distinction: first in the churches he served, then as state mission secretary, then as director of a southwide co-operative committee, and finally as Executive Secretary of a great Foreign Mission Board reaching out into all continents of the earth.

Truly he has been a world figure with planetary horizon, having personally visited churches and stations in many lands, having encouraged and energized every phase of mission endeavor at home and abroad, having solved many problems and difficulties, having prayed with throbbing fervor and having pleaded with tearful force that all co-operant churches would join more vigorously in winning all men everywhere to Christ.

And now he is an eminent emeritus with laurels circling his brow. His beloved companion is close by his side; "each for the other and both for God," they minister in the church where they were married. Worthily he is climaxing his career by writing volumes of value, including this appealing autobiography.

God bless this honored, happy couple, and long may they linger in the sunset glow of this life, though every ready and alerted for the glory and dawn of Eternal Day!

HIGHT C MOORE

Ridgecrest, North Carolina

II

NOTHING is so interesting as life. No literature is more instructive and inspiring than stories of people who have fulfilled in large measure the purposes of God. "Lives of great men all remind us we can make our lives sublime."

The portrayal of the struggles and achievements of Charles E. Maddry is one of the most fascinating stories I have ever read. Beset by many handicaps, he overcame obstacles which would have dismayed and defeated a less resolute personality. When he was tempted to yield to the pull of the low way, a wise and discerning teacher set his feet on the high way and gave him the vision of the richer life.

The decision to commit himself to the Master Teacher, to seek first the kingdom of God and his righteousness, and to interpret the plans of God as related to his own life, led him to the university, to the seminary, to the pastorate, to the secretaryship—first in his own native state of North Carolina, then in the world mission task of Southern Baptists.

As Executive Secretary of the Foreign Mission Board of the Southern Baptist Convention, he visited all of our mission areas and returned from each with a compassionate appeal to Southern Baptists to carry the message of the crucified and risen Lord to the ends of the earth.

When he began his service as Secretary of the Foreign Mission Board, Southern Baptists were under a crushing debt of one and one-half million dollars for their foreign mission work. No new missionaries were being sent out. Then came the dawn of a new day, when under the leadership of Charles Maddry, Southern Baptists took heart and reinforced the depleted ranks of weary missionaries with eager volunteers equipped for service. They began reducing the debt, and within a dozen years every cent of that indebtedness had been paid. For the first time in the hundred years of the existence of the Foreign Mission Board no interest obligations were incurred. In more than thirty countries we now have nearly three times as many missionaries as we had in the dark days of the early '30's.

I count it a happy privilege to write this word of introduction. For forty years I have had fellowship with this greathearted missionary leader. My affection for him and my appreciation of his glorious service were deepened during the several years of my intimate acquaintance with him while serving as editor of *The Commission.*

The thrilling story of Dr. Maddry's life and labors should be placed in every Baptist home and church library in the territory of the Southern Baptist Convention. It will bless and strengthen everyone who reads its message of conquering courage, overcoming faith, and world-encompassing compassion.

E. C. ROUTH

Lockhart, Texas

I

Early Years

On the last day of December, 1839, my grandfather, Abel Maddry, and Jane Gattis, daughter of Alexander Gattis, a Revolutionary hero and a ruling elder in New Hope Presbyterian Church, were married. Abel stole his bride and carried her away riding behind him on a horse. Sixty years later when I asked my great uncle, Samuel, why my great-grandfather had objected to the marriage of Abel and Jane, he said that his father, an old-fashioned, bluestocking Presbyterian, did not believe that the Baptists and the Methodists were very respectable in a religious way. Though he considered young Abel a man of splendid character, hard-working, and possessed of exemplary habits, he could not reconcile himself to the idea of his daughter's taking a husband who belonged to the despised, hard-headed sect of fervent, shouting, evangelistic newcomers who were known as Baptists.

They began housekeeping in a three-room log structure on the "Tailor Gattis" farm, two and one-half miles north of Chapel Hill on the old Hillsboro Road. Here my father was born on May 5, 1841, and was named William Alexander—for his great-grandfather, William Betts, and his grandfather, Alexander Gattis.

Grandfather Maddry was a hard-working man; and, in spite of the thin and rocky soil upon which he had located, he always made a good living. He became a substantial citizen and won for himself a place of high esteem in the Mount Moriah Baptist Church, where he served for more than fifty years as a faithful and devoted deacon. Before the Civil War he was captain of the militia. I remember as a small lad hearing the older people talk of the "Muster Days," when all the township came out after the crops were laid by and spent the day in drilling the young men in military tactics, marksmanship, and other warlike preparations. On these occasions there were social gatherings and athletic contests such as climbing a greased pole, catching a greased pig, shooting at the "bull's eye" for turkeys and pigs, sack racing, and wrestling.

I have examined carefully the old minute or record books of many country Baptist churches. It is significant that almost without exception the slave members are always referred to as "servants" and never as "slaves." I have a marked conviction that our fathers, although they accepted or acquiesced in the institution of human slavery and fought the Civil War to preserve it, in their relationship as brothers in Christ in the churches could not bring themselves to the practice of referring to slaves as such but always as servants. There must have been an innate sense of decency and a feeling of a common brotherhood of equality in Christ that made it incongruous to refer to their black brothers and sisters in Christ, held in bondage against their wills, as slaves.

From the time of the organization of the church at Mount Moriah in 1823, there was a large number of "servants" in the membership. About 1850, the problem of discipline as it related to the large and ever-growing number of Negro members became so demanding and acute that the church elected a colored deacon to assist the white deacons in the handling of all matters concerning the moral and spiritual welfare of the slave contingent in the church.

After the Civil War, Grandfather was looked upon by the newly-freed black people as their friend and defender. Before the war the slaves had been members of Mount Moriah Church, but in 1868 there was full agreement by all the members, white and black, that the time had come for the Negro members of the church to take letters of dismissal and form their own church. Grandfather was made chairman of a committee to help organize and guide the Negro church during the early and difficult days of its beginnings. Several months after the new church, Mount Sinai, was started, a delegation of Negro deacons, sent by the church, came to seek his counsel in a dispute among the brethren over the command of Jesus, "Drink ye all of it." Some of the members had contended that this meant that all the wine brought to the communion table must be drunk, while others had contended that it meant that all the members were to partake of the wine. The contention became sharp, and bitterness in the congregation flared to dangerous proportions. Grandfather set the brethren straight on the matter of the Lord's Supper; henceforth, everything at Sinai was quiet and peaceful!

Grandmother, in keeping with her training in an orthodox Presbyterian home of that day, believed strictly in keeping the Lord's Day holy. All work on the farm had to be finished by Saturday noon; all washing, ironing, and cooking were completed before sundown on Saturday. "Loaf bread," as it was called, was baked in a deep oven before an open fire on Saturday morning. Meats were boiled or baked, and all food for the Lord's Day was prepared on Saturday. Nothing was cooked on Sunday except that water was boiled for the making of the coffee. The children grew up in devotion to the gospel of Christ, and the reading of the Word of God was the natural and accepted practice, not only in this home but in most of the homes in the community.

Mrs. Cornelia Phillips Spencer, eminent North Carolina historian, once said that the University at Chapel Hill was like a great lighthouse sending out its beneficent and illuminating rays into every nook and corner of the state, but that at the base it was dark. The observation of Mrs. Spencer was true to the facts. I was born and grew to manhood at the "base." My father's farm was located three miles north of the university village on the old Hillsboro Road, known in recent years as the Airport Road.

On this poor, rocky farm of ninety acres, nestling at the eastern base of Nunn's Mountain, I first saw the light of day on April 10, 1876, in a three-room log house, situated in a large grove of beautiful oaks and hickories. Two sisters had already come to bless the humble home. There were six more to follow, until nine in all (five girls and four boys) had come to crowd the little log house almost to suffocation. One girl died in infancy; eight grew to adulthood.

In the decade of the 1840's, North Carolina had passed the first public school law. The counties of the state were divided into large school districts; under the law, a schoolhouse was built somewhere near the center of each district. Within a half-mile of my grandfather's home, Strain's schoolhouse was erected. The huge chimney was on the inside of the house and had an open fireplace six feet wide. The neighbors joined in building this first schoolhouse for the community; some gave logs, some lumber, and all contributed the necessary labor.

The house was furnished with rough seats made of oak slabs with holes bored in them. Legs fashioned from pieces of split timber were inserted into the holes. On each side of the house one log was cut out, and a board was fastened over the opening with leather hinges. This provided light and air. The school, in session for some two months after the "crops were laid by," or during January and February, was taught by some itinerant schoolmaster, who usually boarded around with his pupils, spending a week at a time with the leading farmers of the community.

The curriculum of the school was usually limited to the three R's—"reading, 'rit'n, and 'rithmetic." Webster's "Blue-back Speller," then in vogue, was the mainstay for seekers after learning. Usually the school session was far too short for much to be accomplished.

Through the years of my boyhood and youth we had a varied succession of teachers—some good, some poor, and a few who never should have tried to teach. When I was ten years old, there came as teacher for the summer months a young man who was a promising senior at the University. It was his first school and he did *not* believe in "sparing the rod and spoiling the child."

We had two spelling classes—the "little spelling class" and the "big spelling class." I belonged to the former. There was a spirited contest as to who should get the most "head marks." Three of us were far out in the lead—Norman, Minnie, and myself. I was very fond of Minnie, and she professed a decided liking for me. On this particular day Minnie was at the head of the long line; I was second; Norman was third. The teacher gave Minnie a word she could not spell. She stuttered and stumbled and in her desperation telegraphed me out of the corner of her mouth, "How do you spell it?" I was on a hot spot! Conscience and self-interest said, "Don't tell her." Romance and the appeal of those blue eyes said, "Help her out." I threw discretion to the wind and whispered the fatal answer that was to be my undoing. She spelled the word, and it would have passed unnoticed, but Norman cried out, "Charlie told her how to spell it!"

If the teacher had asked me, I feel sure I would have come clean and confessed. Instead, he turned to the young flame of my heart and demanded sternly, "Did he tell you how to spell that word?" Frightened and confused, she replied, "Mr. Blank, I hope I may die if he did." Now that was a poser! What was a gallant gentleman to do when the lady of his heart was in trouble? The outcome? Well, they proved it on me in spite of the protestations of innocence on the part of the two guilty parties!

Mr. Blank sent one of the older boys out for a "turn" of long slender dogwood switches. It was a cool rainy day in August, and I was wearing a coat, which he ordered me to take off. With vigor and evident enjoyment he laid thirty-two lashes upon my all but bare back and legs. Some of the big boys did the counting. I lost count after the first few strokes.

My father, who was one of the school committeemen, was away when I reached home. Mother, with sympathetic tenderness, treated my lacerated and bleeding back with simple home remedies. I remember being wakened from troubled sleep sometime in the night to see Mother holding an oil lamp, while Father examined my bleeding, swollen back and legs.

There was a violent scene early the next morning at the home of the neighbor where the teacher boarded. Father went over to give him a thrashing. However, he would not fight and decided flight was the better part of valor. In a few days, hot tempers cooled, apologies were offered and accepted, and I was sent back to school; but there was no more whipping of little boys that session. Later, the young man graduated from the University and became a prominent college professor.

Through all the years of my teens and early manhood, the bitter memory of that brutal flogging in the old country school lingered, and I promised myself that I would thrash George Blank if I ever met him again.

Then, in the unfolding years, Christ came into my life and took out of my heart all the bitterness and hatred toward the teacher of those boyhood days. I became a preacher and, after the studies at the seminary, came to Greensboro, North Carolina, as pastor of two mission churches. It had been just twenty years since the "battle" at Strain's schoolhouse. Coming out of the post office one day after my arrival in Greensboro, I met a tall, distinguished-looking gentleman—my old teacher. He hesitated, seeming much embarrassed, and then said, "Is this Mr. Maddry?" After I assured him that he had guessed correctly, he said, "Twenty years ago this summer I wronged you greatly. I was brutal and unjust to you, and my conscience has troubled me over this matter all these years. I read in the paper that you had come to a pastorate in our city, and when I saw you, I guessed you were the man. I promised myself that the first time I met you I would apologize for the wrong I did you and ask for your forgiveness."

With emotion he extended his hand. I grasped it gladly and said, "Mr. Blank, if I had met you some years ago, I am afraid there would have been a different story to tell. But the Lord took all the anger and bitterness of that unfortunate incident out of my heart, and I forgave you for the wrong you did me long ago. I now have nothing but love and good wishes for you." We parted with mutual esteem and a good understanding, both glad that we had come face to face and settled the old score between us in the right way.

A Great Teacher

Before I was in my teens there came to live in the community a young bride who was well educated, gentle, and refined; she was a Christian, humble in spirit, and deeply consecrated. She was possessed by a divine urge to uplift the moral, economic, and religious life of the community, though the vast majority of us did not want to be "uplifted." Most of the people had grown accustomed to their grinding poverty and did not want to be disturbed. They resented any new and "hifalutin" plans for uplift and progress. They were backward, poor, and illiterate. Possibly a third of the population could not read or write. They wrested a meager living from the thin and rocky soil. Life was a daily struggle to make ends meet.

The churches were backward, and the "meeting houses" were one-room, "cigar-box" buildings, ugly and unpainted. They were wholly inadequate for teaching or worship. The pastors, in the main, were poorly educated and without qualities of inspiring leadership, although there were notable exceptions. Some were men of fine personality and good natural ability. However, the poverty of the people and lack of support on the part of the churches forced them into secular employment to earn a living. They were absentee preachers instead of being forceful leaders in the churches.

In our home newspapers were few. With the exception of the large family Bible and a precious copy of *The Pilgrim's Progress*, books were scarce.

The newcomer among us did her best to lift up a worthy standard of morals, decency, and high idealism for this ultra-conservative, self-satisfied community. Although she was a Presbyterian, since there was no church of her faith in the community, she threw herself wholeheartedly into the life and activity of the local Methodist church.

The "problem class" in the Sunday school was the boys' class, composed of lads ranging in age from ten to sixteen years. We were known as bad boys, and we prided ourselves on the status the name implied. Some members of the group were possibly more promising than the rest. They were able to read and write. To the others, the printed page was a sealed mystery.

"Miss Joe," as the bride was known to her friends, asked for the privilege of teaching this class. The superintendent, greatly relieved, granted her request. The new teacher was attractive in personality, ardent, and hopeful in spirit. She loved boys and had infinite patience and an unflagging faith in the "comeout'" of a bad boy. She taught the fundamental and essential truths of the Word of God and instilled in some of us a sense of sin and a longing for a better life in Christ. She loved us, prayed for us, held on to us, never gave us up. She tried to teach us the rudiments of decency and good manners. Yet we were not conscious at the time that she was doing anything for us, and I am sure she herself was often discouraged and ready to give up. When I was about seventeen years of age, she moved away from the community and went with her invalid husband to live in Florida.

Full twenty years passed by, and it gradually dawned on me that I owed an eternal debt of gratitude to this faithful and devoted Sunday school teacher. We had lost touch with each other, but through friends in the old community, news came that she had "fallen on evil days." Age and infirmity had crept on apace, and poverty had come to cast its darkening shadow over her declining years.

There came over me a strong feeling that I should go to Florida, seek out this devoted teacher of the long ago, and tell her before it was too late how much I loved her and appreciated all she had meant to me in my formative years.

Securing a ten-days' vacation from my church, I journeyed to Florida and found her living in a very humble home in the pine barrens of her adopted state. She was still cheerful and courageous. Dire poverty had not dampened her ardor nor quenched her passion for the high and holy things in Christ. She was overjoyed to see me, and I spent two nights and a glorious Sunday in that humble home, in sweet fellowship and blessed joy, as we recounted the sacred memories of the years of long ago.

In a few months she slipped away to the better land; but the holy memory of her prayers, her teaching, her love, and her faith abide with me.

Ex-slaves had settled on the marginal lands all about our neighborhood. Most of them had bought little, poor, rocky patches of land and were trying to make a living. My grandfather was always a friend and a helper of the Negro people; they looked up to him and went to him with all of their troubles and sorrows. My father followed in his footsteps. For many years he was a school committeeman for the Negro district school near us and did all he could to help provide the Negroes with a schoolhouse and with funds for their school. He did his best to encourage and help them in every way. Every Negro in all the countryside believed in the justice and fair dealing of my father.

Very few of these ex-slaves could read or write, though some who were born in slavery just before the end of the Civil War had learned to read and write in a very limited way. However, since almost all of them were ambitious that their children should get all the education possible, they sent them to school for the two months the public school ran during the year. The schoolhouse was a miserable log cabin, and the teacher was very poorly paid; but the poverty-stricken black people were doing their best to educate and train their children in the things of decency and religion.

Almost all the Negroes I knew in the township were Baptists and were loyal to their church and to their preacher. The title for the preacher was "Reverend," and, if worthy, he was held in high esteem by his people. Reverend L. H. Hackby was pastor of the Negro Baptist church in Chapel Hill for more than forty years. He was a tall, handsome, distinguished-looking man with a high forehead, a long straight nose, and thin lips. Well educated and with a splendid reputation for honesty in all public dealings, he stood for everything that was good for the people in general and for the race in particular. He was a dignified man, and every white person who knew him respected him. He was really a very gifted preacher and orator, and the Lord used him in a marvelous way in leading the Negroes around Chapel Hill in everything that made for character, decency, and order. He was also a splendid schoolteacher and taught along with his preaching. He was truly one of God's noblemen.

I was fourteen and a half years old before I ever had a ready-made suit of clothes. In the spring of 1890, my father gave me half a bag of fertilizer and an acre of thin, rocky land for a "cotton patch." I planted that cotton and cultivated it with loving care. The yield was poor, and the price was low; for the cotton and seed I got only fifteen dollars, but I was rich beyond the dreams of Croesus!

In company with a cousin, who was a year older than I, and a self-confident sixteen-year-old neighbor boy who had boasted of his ability to get the better of the sharpest merchant in a trade, I went to Durham, then a sprawling market town of some five thousand inhabitants, to buy my first suit of "store clothes." We drove twelve miles over a wretched road in a one-horse wagon drawn by a little mule. The trip took three hours.

We spent two hours bargaining and haggling with a Jewish merchant over the price and finally bought for seven dollars and fifty cents each, two suits just alike, one for my cousin and one for myself. A stiff-bosomed shirt with a detachable collar, a ready-tied blue striped cravat, and a hat completed the most gorgeous and satisfying outfit that ever adorned the person of an awkward, gangling, self-conscious, fourteen-year-old country boy!

Sunday school met at nine-thirty the next morning, but I was on the church grounds a full hour before to show off my new outfit. In the afternoon I went to see my first girl. She was twenty years old, gentle and pretty, and the most popular and sought-after young woman in the neighborhood. The fact that she was already engaged to be married did not lessen my love for her in the slightest! I took her some cheap candy, which she received with the gracious charm which characterized her conduct toward everyone.

My mother, a woman of boundless energy, was tireless in her efforts to see to it that her family was adequately clothed and properly care for. She hated poverty, but she was compelled to struggle against its galling and humiliating ravages all through the years of her married life until she was sixty years of age. Her father, who had succeeded at several callings and made money, was indulgent with his family and a good provider. He was very generous toward my mother, and when she married he set her up with all that was needed for housekeeping. Beautiful and substantial pieces of walnut furniture have come down to her children of this day—all the gifts of my grandfather to his favorite daughter, Julia Rebecca. He gave her ninety acres of land, as good eighty years ago as any other farm in the community.

However, my father was not a success as a farmer. Prosperity did not come to the young Maddry couple. He was a young man of great promise when he came to his majority in 1861. His education was above the average of his companions in the community, and he was ready to enter college when the Civil War interrupted his plans. He told me the last time I ever saw him alone that he felt God had called him to preach. He came home from the war defeated, his health gone; and he went through life with a sense of frustration resting upon him.

By the time I was fifteen, I was compelled by force of circumstances to take the lead in most of the activities of the farm. Under Mother's direction, I did much of the marketing as well as the peddling of fruit, vegetables, chickens, wood, and other farm products from house to house in the near-by village. My mother was not an exception, but like the other housewives in the community, she carded the cotton, spun the thread, and knitted all the socks and stockings worn by the family. As my sisters grew older, they lightened the burden in every possible way, but the responsibility always remained upon my mother's shoulders. Mother made our clothes by hand—coats, pants, dresses, and underwear of all kinds. I was in my early teens before the family was able to buy a sewing machine or a cook stove.

All of the family except Mother and the smaller children worked in the fields during crop times. From the time I was fifteen years of age, I went out to work for the neighboring farmers at harvest time and during rush seasons. In the summer I worked in the tobacco fields cutting, housing, and curing tobacco. In the winter when the snow was not too deep, I cut cord wood. In the late fall, I cut the winter's supply of fire wood for several of the older people in the community who were unable to cut their own. The current price for this labor was forty cents a day and board.

One of the neighbors had the contract for supplying a part of the fuel for the little wood-burning engine that hauled the freight and passengers over the University railroad which ran the ten miles from Chapel Hill to University Station on the main line of the Richmond and Danville Railway. He paid fifty cents a cord for the cutting of this wood, and the worker boarded himself. The long slender pines were felled, cut into two-foot lengths, split, and put into cords two feet high and sixteen feet long. No one had ever heard of an eight-hour day in 1890. If I worked hard from sunrise to sunset, I could cut and put up a cord of wood—all for fifty cents.

After "laying by" the crop in the summer of 1893, at seventeen I secured a job as section hand on the University branch of the Richmond and Danville Railway. The section master was Cad R. Williams of Chapel Hill. He was a considerate Christian gentleman, always treating the men under him with justice tempered with kindness. He died in 1953 at an advanced age. He had been an active and useful deacon in the Carrboro Baptist Church for many years. He was my life-long friend from the day I went to work under him, fifty-six years ago.

Religious Influences in Early Childhood

Eno Baptist Church, organized by Elders Samuel Harris and Rubin Pickett, was constitued in 1773 and for seventy-five years was a flourishing and influential body. Elder John McCabe was the first pastor. The tide of immigration flowing into Granville and Orange Counties prior to the Revolution from the eastern counties of Virginia, especially Isle of Wight, Surry, and Northampton Counties, swelled the church membership at Eno to imposing proportions.

The "arms" or daughters that went out from Eno, the old mother church, around 1862, became strong, missionary churches. They all espoused the cause of missions and progress and aligned themselves with the newly-organized Baptist State Convention in 1830. They have grown and prospered through the one hundred and twenty years since the split took place. Eno, the mother church, which cast her lot with the anti-missionary group of Baptist churches, is only a pathetic memory.

"Patterson's Meeting House" was an "arm" of the Eno Church and later became known as Mount Moriah Baptist Church. It was located some five miles northeast of our home on the Chapel Hill–Oxford highway. The church was organized in 1823 by Elders Fairhill and Farthing, "by order of the Eno Church."

Before 1850, the Methodists in Chapel Hill belonged to the Orange Methodist Church congregation, a flourishing and influential group. In the decade of the 1850's, a Methodist church was organized in Chapel Hill, and the members who lived in town took their church membership into the new village church.

Owing to the fact the Mount Moriah Baptist Church, the home church of the Maddry family for three generations, was five miles distant over roads that were often impassable for six months in the year, the children attended Sunday school at Orange Methodist Church. For some years, Grandfather Abel Maddry, who always went to his own church the first Sunday in each month, was at intervals superintendent of the Sunday school at Orange Church. My father often taught a class, and later on in my early manhood, I taught there at various times.

Orange Methodist Church has given to the ministry four native sons—three Methodists and one Baptist. In the decade of the 1840's, my great-uncle, Reverend Alexander Gattis, Jr., the youngest son of Alexander, the Revolutionary patriot and ruling elder in New Hope

Presbyterian Church, was prominent in the work of the North Carolina Methodist Conference.

The most distinguished son of Orange Methodist Church was the Reverend Samuel B. Turrentine, who graduated from the University of North Carolina in the class of 1884 and became pastor of several of the largest Methodist churches in the state. The crowning of his long ministry was his work as president of Greensboro College, a historic and excellent Methodist school for women, located in Greensboro, North Carolina.

Our church at Mount Moriah had preaching only once a month. The other Sundays we attended Orange Church, New Hope, and other near-by churches. One by one, as the children were converted, they went with my father to Mount Moriah Baptist Church.

My mother's people were Methodists. On the Gattis side of the family, they were Presbyterians. My grandmother, Jane Gattis Maddry, wife of Abel Maddry, was a Presbyterian for some time after they were married. She then voluntarily joined the church at Mount Moriah with my grandfather. When I was five or six years old, my mother was converted at Orange Methodist Church and offered herself for membership in this congregation. When the pastor, going down the line of converts, asked Mother how she wanted to be baptized, she said, "By immersion." The pastor was nonplussed for the moment but recovered himself and said, "All right, Sister Maddry, we'll appoint a time and come out and baptize you." Nothing further was heard of the matter of Mother's baptism for several months. One day Father came back from Chapel Hill and said to Mother, "I saw your pastor, and he said for you to bring Brother Gattis (a steward) with you to Old Field Creek next Thursday afternoon, and he will baptize you." Mother said nothing as she went about her work. Before the day appointed for her baptism by the Methodist pastor, I heard her say to Father, "If they're ashamed to baptize me on Sunday when the neighbors can come and see the baptism, I'll go with you to Mount Moriah where they're not ashamed to baptize me."

It went along this way for some years; I do not know exactly how long, but on the fourth Sunday in September, 1887, Mother and I were baptized at the same time by Reverend John C. Hocutt in Patterson's Mill, New Hope Creek, near Mount Moriah Baptist Church. I was eleven years old. I remember that it was a cold, chilly day. A great throng of people gathered on the sloping hillside overlooking the mill pond, and the pastor baptized four candidates.

After the baptism, we repaired to the church, and after the sermon, the church observed the Lord's Supper. I remember my grandfather passing the elements. Father and Grandfather, along with all the church members, came down the line, as they did in the old days, extending the right hand of fellowship to all new members.

New Hope Presbyterian Church, organized about 1760, was five miles north from my home on the Hillsboro road. It was surrounded by a great forest. The first building was of logs and octagonal in shape. There were port holes for rifle fire in the event of Indian attacks. In those early days the congregation would meet and stack their guns outside. Some of the members would be left on guard to give warning of attack from the Indians. For one hundred and ninety years this church has been a very active and vigorous religious force in the life of south Orange County.

In my boyhood we often attended services at New Hope. Their ministers were always cultured and well trained for the work of the ministry. They often lacked the evangelistic fervor and emotional appeal of the Methodist and Baptist ministers of the day, but they were well versed in the teaching of the Scriptures.

For more than fifty years after the founding of the University, there was no Presbyterian church in Chapel Hill. The members of this faith in the village affiliated with the church at New Hope, eight miles away. Dr. James Phillips, noted teacher in the University and the father of Mrs. Cornelia Phillips Spencer, was for many years a leading member of this church and pastor for a generation.

In his boyhood my father often attended this church. There was no means of heating the churches in those early days before the Civil War. The people attended the services faithfully in all sorts of weather and sat patiently through the service, which often lasted for two hours. Dr. Phillips in the "long prayer" often held forth for forty minutes (the congregation standing), and the sermon that followed always went on beyond an hour. Dr. Charles Phillips, son of the long-time pastor and a noted teacher in the University, was also pastor at New Hope for many years.

In addition to these churches of my boyhood, the Hardshell Baptists had occasional preaching at a near-by schoolhouse, known as Piney Mountain. There were several Hardshell families in this community. The pastor would come out from Durham and preach once a month in the afternoon. He was usually a carpenter, farmer, or a mechanic. None of their pastors gave all their time to the ministry. As a rule they were uneducated men and received no stated salary from their congregations. They were rigid Calvinists and believed that they were the one and only true church. They preached in a sing-song tone of voice, the "holy tone," a practice they continue even to the present day. Very few of the young people join the Hardshell churches until later in life. One must have a tremendous religious experience, a vision, or a dream, before he can be admitted to a Hardshell church.

Baptist churches in my boyhood gave strict attention to the conduct of the membership. They met once a month, on Saturday, for worship and purposes of discipline. There was very little business to attend to except the matter of inquiring into the conduct of the church family during the previous month. The pastor would preach for an hour or more, and then call the church into conference. If the pastor was absent, the leading deacon would read the Scripture, comment thereon, lead in prayer, and call the church into conference. Many churches required that every male member should attend and answer roll call every three months or be subject to discipline. The female members were required to attend and answer roll call only once a year. Our church had several hundred members. It was quite a task to call the roll and check the answer of each individual as to his church attendance. When about sixteen years of age, I was cited to the church for non-attendance. After explaining that my father compelled me to stay home and plow following a good rain while the land was "in season," the pastor, who was moderator, said, "The young brother is excused." I felt as if I had escaped a term in the penitentiary!

Drunkenness was considered wholly unbecoming in the conduct of a church member. After being warned several times, the member was excluded from the fellowship of the church if he repeated the offense. It was considered a great disgrace to be "turned out" of the church for drunkenness. It was the duty of the members of the church, especially the deacons, to report all matters of misconduct on the part of the membership. Sometimes a church trial would last for months before it was finished.

Most of the country churches in my boyhood had Sunday schools. A few of the pious elders of the church, men and women, met with the young people and children and conducted a Sunday school, doing the best they could to teach them the Word of God. A great majority of the church members did not attend the Sunday school. A literature of sorts could be had from the publishing houses of some of the denominations, but the lesson helps of those early days were very poor and inadequate. The Bible was the main text book. Faithful men and women explained to the boys and girls the Word of God and the plan of salvation. Many of the older members of the church were well grounded in the Scriptures. They knew the fundamentals of salvation, and they loved young people. Some of them were devoted teachers, and with little to assist them in the way of class rooms and literature, they were faithful in teaching the Sunday school pupils.

There were no organizations in the church for the training of the young people in those days. Sometimes during the summer months, led by a faithful deacon appointed by the church, the young people would have a prayer meeting on Sunday evening. There were always some carping critics in our church who did not believe that the church house ought to be used for meetings of the young people because they were afraid that something would be done that was unseemly or disorderly. However, to the credit of our pastor and church, they were willing to designate one deacon to meet with us and give general direction and supervision to our efforts to secure training in the matter of conducting public meetings, speaking, and leading in prayer. The meetings, of course, were largely social. The young people had no other outlet for their activities and no other place of meeting for social intercourse save in the young people's prayer meeting, the Sunday school, or at the church meeting.

II

A Discovery and a Decision

One day in January, 1894, when there was snow on the ground, I was splitting pine logs in a new piece of ground we were clearing for tobacco. My younger brother came to the "new ground" with a message from Mother saying that a schoolteacher had come to see my father, who was then chairman of the local school committee of the Strain school district. Since Father was away from home, the visitor wanted to see me. I quit my work and went to see what he wanted.

The stranger introduced himself as J. P. Canaday, a student who had come up from Johnston County to study in the University. He explained that he was a teacher in his home county and had entered the University with the purpose of preparing himself to do better work in his chosen calling. He explained further that he had a wife and three small children, and that since his funds were being exhausted, he was forced to leave the University and seek employment to support his family. As it was mid-winter, the public schools of his native county were already supplied with teachers, and he was seeking a vacancy in some school in Orange County. It had come to his attention that the Strain school district had been unable to secure a teacher for the two and one-half months' term.

He had already seen one of the school committeemen and had been told that the committee had about decided to postpone the school session until the next summer. He wanted to urge me to intercede with my father to give him the school and suggested that since it was two months before "plow time," he would be happy to have me under his instruction for that time. I explained that I was eighteen years of age and did not propose to attend school any more. He asserted with confidence that if he secured the school, he would be delighted to have me as one of his students, and that he believed I would be interested in his method of instruction and would find it profitable.

I confess that I was impressed with the man and convinced by his confident assurance that it was not too late for me to go to school and secure an education. His earnest sincerity and gentle spirit won my heart, and in thirty minutes I was his willing disciple. When he left, I had pledged him my loyalty and support in his efforts to secure the school.

The outcome of the matter was that a majority of the committee voted to give Mr. Canaday the school. All my plans were changed. I decided to enter school and pursue further the undertaking of trying to prepare myself for something in life beyond the occupation of rail splitter and small farmer.

I realize now, after sixty years, that this seemingly casual meeting with a stranger on that winter morning was a crucial moment of my life. I was to discover that the six weeks spent under his instruction would mean more to me than all I had received in the haphazard years of school I had attended since I was five years of age.

Mr. Canaday's method of teaching, was different from that of any teacher I had ever known. Secondary with him were the formal lessons in the few inadequate text books we possessed. His fund of information and knowledge appeared to be unlimited. Interesting and inspiring, he seemed to "speak with authority."

He organized a debating society, and once a week he had speeches and recitations by his pupils. Once each day he had everyone lay aside books, and he made a talk on some historic event or described to us some battle, encouraging us to ask questions and make comments. He outlined some of the great books in literature and recited for us some of the great poems of the English world. He seemed never to tire, and the well-spring of his inspiration never ran dry. It mattered not that his pupils were ignorant, poor, and uninspiring; he was always the same fascinating, uplifting personality, pouring out his best to the small group who gathered about him in that bare log schoolhouse.

I was one of the "big boys" in school. One day toward the close of that first session we took a walk in the oak forest beyond the spring. When we turned to go back to the schoolhouse, he stopped and faced me suddenly with this startling question: "What are you going to do with your life?" I was dumb and silent for a moment, but when I could find my voice, I replied that I supposed I would farm a few acres of rocky Orange County soil just as my fathers had done for a hundred and fifty years since they first found their way from Scotland

and settled on Presswood Creek. He asked why I did not prepare myself for entrance into the University, located less than three miles away. I was startled at the suggestion. All my life I had heard the ringing of the University bell calling the students to classes every hour of the day, but this was the first time anyone had ever suggested that the University existed for such as I.

Finally, I managed to stammer, in my surprise, that I was already a grown man, that I lacked money or influence, and that I could never prepare for entrance into the University. I said, furthermore, that this great institution was for the rich and important of the state and was far beyond my dreams or even the wildest flight of my imagination. To all of this my teacher replied that it was not a wild dream but wholly within the realm of the possible. His eyes seemed to pierce my soul as he said, "You can do it. You have something in you. I have been watching you these weeks and studying your possibilities. I am convinced that God has something great in store for you—something far beyond anything you have ever dreamed. You can do it. There is no difficulty that cannot be overcome if only you will give yourself to the undertaking with all your mind and soul and strength."

I was silent as we made our way back to the schoolhouse. This little man had profoundly stirred my soul and kindled my imagination. He had lighted a flame in me that has never gone out. Henceforth life held new meaning, for from that hour a new purpose dominated my life. He was the first ever to tell me that there was something in my life worth striving for and that God is always ready to help those who try to help themselves.

This was truly a revolutionary hour. As I followed the winding mountain path along the banks of Presswood Creek to my home that afternoon, new dreams were born in my soul. New ambitions and enthusiasms took possession of my being. This good Barnabas, full of faith and the Holy Spirit, had found me and set my feet in a new path.

In the spring of 1896 I was twenty years of age. After finishing "laying by" the crops, my father informed me that he was "setting me free" and that he would give me the rest of my time until I was twenty-one years of age. He expressed the hope that I would be able to go to school but said that he was then unable to help me to that end. I replied that I was going to go to school if there were any possible way to finance the undertaking.

Just at that time I read an announcement in the *Chapel Hill News* that Professor J. W. Canada of Summerfield, Guilford County, North Carolina, was going to open a preparatory school in Chapel Hill around September the first. I immediately wrote Mr. Canada telling him of my desire to enter his school to prepare for the University. I had a letter from him in a few days saying that he would come to see me. About the middle of July Mr. Canada came out, and we talked over the possibility of entering his school in September. I told him frankly that I had no money and would have to work my way. He offered to give me my tuition, which amounted to $3.00 per month, if I would cut the wood and make the fires in some ten or twelve stoves and fireplaces in the old dwelling house that he had rented for the school building. I accepted his offer and on the first of September entered the school. It was one of many preparatory schools that through the years had sprung up in Chapel Hill and flourished for a season and then passed away. However, in the providence of God, this school came at the right time for me.

I walked three miles to the village every day, leaving my home about sunup or earlier, and cut wood until the bell rang for school at 9:00 o'clock. In the afternoon from 4:00 until 6:00 I cut wood again and then walked three miles to my home. I was a grown man, long and lank. I entered classes with boys and girls who were twelve and fourteen years of age. The first year I took subjects such as grammar, arithmetic, North Carolina history, United States history, physiology, and physics, often sitting up until midnight studying by the dim light of an oil lamp. My mother prepared my lunch of whatever happened to be at hand, and sometimes it was very poor and skimpy. I felt awkward and greatly humiliated to have to go into the classes of small boys and girls and start at the very bottom.

However, there was one teacher in the school, Mrs. Sally Mae Wilson, of Virginia, who was like a mother to me. She was a great person with a wonderful gift of inspiring ambitious students to get an education. She helped me in every way, correcting my faults privately and making suggestions concerning all matters of conduct, social etiquette, personal appearance, and habits of study. She seemed to take a special delight in helping me overcome my many handicaps as I struggled toward preparation for the University. I was a very unpromising specimen, and I am sure that her patience was often tried. However, I was ambitious to learn and had an insatiable thirst for knowledge. One thing in my favor was that I had read a great deal of history. As a boy, I had read all the books in the community and ranged far and wide borrowing books and reading everything I could find. Of course, there had been no system or method in my reading, but I had read widely, and I found that this gave me an advantage over the smaller boys and girls in my classes. In a few months I began to write and found that I could master new subjects. I had never seen a Latin book until I entered preparatory school and, in fact, did not know that such things as dead languages could be studied in modern schools. I went through the courses offered by the school in two years, doing the work usually requiring four years. I graduated in the spring of 1898 with a certificate of entrance to the University with the exception of Latin. I had to go back to this high school three times a week during the first year at the University to take Latin. A new world had opened to me, and I entered it with eagerness and enthusiasm.

Some quick, alert, self-confident fellows made good money during the summer months selling stereoscopes and pictures. I was wholly on my own and was compelled to accept any honorable employment I could find. A representative of one of the big national companies came to the University in the spring of 1898 to engage and train prospective agents. Having finished high school in May, I signed up, along with a number of others, to take the brief and intensive training course offered for salesmen. The representative knew his business. He had an attractive and engaging personality and easily persuaded us that the people out in the rural areas were ready and anxious to buy pictures. The harvest was ripe and wasting for the lack of reapers, and we were to go out with joy and enthusiasm to bring in the golden grain! The agent gave us intensive training in the art and technique of picture salesmanship. The approach, getting into the home, sensing the member of the household who was yearning to buy pictures—these points were all explained.

It seemed so thrilling and easy! There was to be no more worry in the fall about money for entrance fees, books, board, or other college expenses! There was plenty to be had in the picture business! Three months were ahead—June, July, and August—in which to reap the golden harvest awaiting eager and enthusiastic men out there among the natives! I was assigned the territory of Wake County, outside Raleigh. Early in June, with a pony and road cart borrowed from my father, I made my way to Auburn in eastern Wake County. On a lovely June morning, I began my career as a picture salesman.

It was the busy season on the farm. Everybody who was big enough to work was busy with household duties or was in the cotton and tobacco fields. Housewives were engaged in the preparation of dinner or with the week's washing. I soon found that peddlers, book agents, fruit tree agents, and picture agents were unwelcome visitors to farm homes on a Monday morning in June!

Before nightfall, it began to dawn on me that the farmers of Wake County were not as eager for stereoscopic pictures of current heroes and great works of art as the agent who trained us had made us believe. By the end of the first week the bitter truth began to penetrate—not only was I in the wrong business, but I was a dismal failure as a picture salesman. My small stock of money was soon gone, and it became increasingly difficult to find a place that would give me shelter for the night. Crackers and cheese purchased at country stores usually satisfied my hunger for lunch. The pony was put on scant rations, also.

Twenty miles east of Raleigh, hungry, tired, and wholly discouraged one afternoon, I tried in vain for several miles along the highway to find a home for the night. It was the same everywhere—the threshers were expected, the baby was sick, or the man of the house was away from home. At some houses the simple statement sufficed: "We never take in agents and peddlers."

The shadows of twilight were falling when I came to a beautiful country home. I had been told along the way, "Mr. Needham Jones lives up the road. Perhaps he would take you in." I hitched my pony at the gate, and with diffidence made my way to the front porch. A fine looking man, obviously a gentleman farmer, and his well-dressed, good-looking wife were sitting on the porch. They greeted me cordially and invited me in. I gave them my name, stated my business, and asked for a night's lodging. I was given a gracious welcome and assured that they would be pleased to have me as a guest for the night.

A servant took my horse, and I was shown to the guest room. Soon a maid brought me a pitcher of iced water, and I was told that the supper bell would ring in a few minutes. The supper was excellent and bountiful; the welcome was genuine and gracious.

As I went to sleep that night, just one thought troubled me: "Suppose Mr. Jones should charge me for the night's lodging! How much would it be?" Any amount above a dollar would wipe out my operating capital! It was with apprehension that I asked him next morning how much I owed. To my great relief, he replied that he was glad to have me and that there was no thought of any charge! He invited me to come again at any time and assured me that there would always be a welcome awaiting me.

Thinking that perhaps I would have better success in western Wake County, I transferred my operations to Apex and the section around Olive's Chapel, but there I found the same conditions prevailing. The farmers were busy with their work and wholly disinclined to invest in stereoscopes and pictures. One night it looked very much as if I were going to be compelled to sleep in a straw stack when Mr. Billy Sears, a tobacco planter, took me in and gave me a night's lodging free!

Realizing that I was a complete failure as a salesman, I decided to give up the picture business. In the latter part of June I went back over the same territory to deliver the few orders I had sold. Unable to secure the pony and cart for this second trip, I went to Auburn by train. The weather was very hot, and before the week was out, my feet were blistered and walking was agony. The orders I had taken were filled, and I was able to settle fully with the company. There was enough left over to buy a railroad ticket to Durham, where I found friends and a job more nearly commensurate with my ability.

Mother did my laundry at home each week and sent it the twelve miles by someone coming to market. Week by week, as the days slipped by, I dreamed of what was drawing nearer and nearer—the day when I would enter the University. I laid aside four dollars every week toward the fund necessary for entrance fees and books.

Then came the great temptation. The Spanish-American War was in full blast in the summer of 1898. A volunteer company from Durham was being organized. Enthusiasm was running high, and my first cousin, J. Frank Maddry, volunteered. Since he was a newspaper man, there was much in the papers concerning the bravery and gallantry of the Durham Company. Fear was widespread that the war would be over before the Durham Company could reach Cuba and strike a powerful and decisive blow for the downtrodden people so long oppressed by the cruel Spaniards!

I was sorely tempted to join up with these crusaders for freedom, although I knew that Mother would bitterly oppose my plans if she heard of them. She had lived through the horrors of one war and the blight of reconstruction which followed; she had lived for thirty years with a sick and defeated ex-soldier of that unnecessary and unfortunate struggle. When I went home for a brief visit one

Sunday, she reminded me that for years I had been striving and planning for the day when I could enter the University. That day, long anticipated, was just a month away. If I turned aside now, the one chance of a lifetime would be gone for me. In all probability I would be killed, or if I did come back, my health might be ruined and I would spend a miserable lifetime in regret that I had thrown away my one great opportunity.

Somehow, in the light of Mother's entreaties and determined opposition, the glamor and glory that seemed to await me in Cuba began to take on a pale and sickly hue. Before going back to Durham that evening, I had given her my sacred promise that I would let the Durham Company get along the best they could without my help.

On September 1, I gave up my job, settled my debts, bought some badly needed clothing, and proceeded to Chapel Hill to enter the University. When all necessary items had been paid, I found to my consternation that I had one ten dollar bill left from all my summer's work.

I applied to the faculty committee which had supervision of Commons Hall for a waiter's job. About fifteen men were given their board of eight dollars per month for waiting on ten men each. The work was light, and the jobs were much sought after. I failed to get the appointment because the committee understood that, if necessary, I could walk the three miles each way daily to my father's home.

However, the faculty decided that walking six miles daily would give me ample exercise, so I was excused from paying the gymnasium fee. The total entrance fees that must be paid amounted to $13.25, and I had only $10.00. Where the remainder was to come from I did not know.

On the day appointed for the registration of freshmen, I walked over to the University and hung around the offices in the South Building all day watching the students register. Late in the evening, I made my way with slow steps and a heavy heart three miles over the hills to my old home. Early next day I was back again guarding with care my ten dollars and a certificate from the Canada High School entitling me to enter the freshman class. Finally late in the day, with a growing sense of despair, I left the campus and made my way to the village, stopping at the corner of Franklin and Henderson streets to greet some friends.

Presently an elderly farmer who had married my father's first cousin came along driving his team of mules. He lived east of town on the Raleigh Road, and in slack times on the farm he hauled cord wood to the members of the faculty and townspeople. He greeted me in his gruff, hearty way, inquiring whether I had entered the University. I told him I did not have enough money for the payment of the entrance fees and had about decided to give up the idea of school. He asked me how much I had and how much was required for entrance fees; when I gave him the information requested, he took out a rusty leather pocket book and handed me five dollars with the injunction to pay it back as soon as I could.

"I haven't got much education," said he, "but I want you to go to the University and make something of yourself. Go and register in the morning, and get down to work." He drew the reins over his mules and was gone.

All the joy bells of heaven were ringing in my soul that evening as I made my way out to Presswood Creek. When the Registrar's Office opened next morning, I was on hand, eager to enter the door of challenge and opportunity that had swung open to me.

In 1898 all University buildings, including offices, classrooms, and dormitories, were heated with wood or coal in individual fireplaces or stoves. There was a central yard where all wood was sawed into proper lengths for stove or fireplace. The wood saw was powered with a small upright engine. J. Edward Latta, an associate of Professor J. W. Gore in the Department of Physics was in charge of the light plant and wood yard. Since Mr. Latta employed some six or eight husky country boys as helpers around the wood saw, I secured a regular job which paid ten cents per hour. My job was to take the cut-off blocks from the saw and throw them on the heap of "long wood or short wood" as the case might be. Ordinarily we worked from two-thirty until dark, but if the weather was cold and the demands for wood heavy, the lights were turned on under the woodshed, and we worked until seven o'clock. Though the work was hard and the pay small, food was cheap, and a little money went a long way. I did my own cooking, and in the spring of 1899, after work, I would often go by Sparrow's butcher shop and buy a pound of beef liver for ten cents.

In February, 1899, came a deep snow, which began at one o'clock on Saturday and continued until Tuesday noon. All classes in the University were suspended for a week, for it was bitterly cold, and the snow was deep. The wood gave out, and the students had trouble keeping warm. Professor Gore, Chairman of the Faculty Committee on Power and Heating, called his "saw boys" together and offered us the amazing wage of twenty cents per hour! We accepted and for ten days were in big money!

Having settled the matter of a "call" to the ministry, I felt it was high time to begin activities in that direction. Since I was already twenty-three years old, I decided to accept every opportunity that came my way to teach in Sunday school or lead prayer meeting. I worked in the union services at Carrboro, taught in the Sunday school at Orange Church, and sang in the choir of the village Baptist Church.

Because the University YMCA was in desperate financial straits, no one would accept the position of treasurer. Allen Barwick, always the gracious and charming gentleman, was president of the "Y." He persuaded me that I had been set apart in a peculiar way to pull the "Y" out of its financial difficulties and thus render an outstanding service to the religious life of the University. Accepting the task of treasurer, I did what could be done to improve a bad situation. In my junior year, I was elected president of a rejuvenated YMCA.

At the turn of the century, the two literary societies, the Dialectic and Philanthropic, still played a major role in the life of the school. Debating was a popular pastime, and intense interest was taken in all inter-society and inter-collegiate contests. After joining the "Di" Society at the first meeting of the session of 1898, I never missed an opportunity of trying to learn something of the art of thinking and of giving expression to my thoughts to any group who would listen. All freshmen were excused from speaking the first night they were on duty. I refused to accept the customary favor extended freshmen, and to the disgust of many upperclassmen who were interested only in an early adjournment, I insisted on making my speech in turn.

Because of debt and lack of necessary funds, I was compelled to drop out of school at the close of the fall term of my senior year. After a year of hard work as county school superintendent and pastor of five churches, I re-entered on January 1 as a member of the class of 1903.

The work of the spring term was very heavy. I maintained an office in the County Court House in Hillsboro, twelve miles away, and went over on Friday nights to attend to school matters on Saturday. I secured a supply for some of the churches of the field until I finished the University in June. I carried on the church work at Hillsboro and near-by Mars Hill, preaching three times each month.

I had taken all the work offered by Professor Horace H. Williams, Professor of Philosophy, including his famous course in logic. His course in comparative religions was especially stimulating and helpful, and part of this course was a discriminating and critical study of the Prophet Isaiah. Under the guidance of Mr. Williams I wrote my graduating thesis on the work of this great Messianic prophet under the title, "The Work of the Prophet in the Religious Life."

Early in the spring term, I decided to enter the contest for the Mangum Medal in Oratory, the most coveted honor offered by the University in that day. The preliminary contest before a committee of the faculty was open to any member of the senior class. The four best speakers were selected to represent the class on commencement day. The winner in the final contest was awarded the coveted medal.

Early in April the committee announced that the preliminary contest would take place on the following Saturday at ten o'clock. I was greatly disappointed because I was compelled to be in the office in Hillsboro every Saturday, attending to school matters. The committee, learning of my desire to enter the contest, generously offered to hold the final decision as to the winners until Monday and give me a chance to be heard. I appeared before the committee, and when the names of the winners were posted on the bulletin board, my name appeared fourth on the list.

Immediately the all-absorbing question was the topic of my speech. Had I made a wise selection? The faculty committee seemed to think so, but two of my teachers and best friends said that I could not win with the speech made before the committee.

Mr. Williams urged me to reshape my thesis on Isaiah and assured me that it would be a winner. Dr. Thomas Hume, head of the Department of English, said that I could not win with Isaiah, but that victory would be mine if I would speak on "The Literary Value of the Psalms of David," this being the gist of a course I had taken under him in advanced English. This did not click with me any more than did Professor Williams' Isaiah.

During the year spent in rural school work in Orange County, I had become greatly interested in and concerned over the terrible lack of adequate schools for the country boys and girls. I saw that on the whole the farmers were far more interested in improving the breed of their hogs, cows, and mules than they were in improving the minds of their boys and girls. When I saw the youth of this backward rural county going through the same hard and bitter experience through which I had passed, I was mightily moved. There was a speech simmering and boiling in my soul that sooner or later must be made. Like the Psalmist, "My heart was hot within me; while I was musing the fire burned: then spake I with my tongue." Going apart one day, in three hours I wrote a speech on "The Duty of the Southland to the Country Boy." Though it was somewhat sophomoric, grandiose, and lacking in substance, it was my very own. I knew I could speak it with conviction and sincerity.

That night I went down to see "Old Horace," as all his boys lovingly called him. I told him I had been having trouble with Isaiah and suggested that he let me read him the winning speech I had written that morning. He fixed himself to hear, and I proceeded to read with satisfaction and confidence. When I had finished reading, he looked at the blank wall for some time and then turned to me with the melancholy look of profound sorrow for which he was famous and said, "Mr. Maddry, you will never win anything with that speech."

I went away with leaden feet.

Nearing the campus, the thought suddenly flashed into my mind: "Why not go and see Dr. Smith, your English teacher, and get his advice? I crossed the street to the fraternity house where he lived. Answering my knock he called out in his jovial voice, "Come in!" I found him in dressing gown and slippers smoking his pipe and reading a book, his feet propped up on his desk.

"Sit down, Mr. Maddry," he said. "What can I do for you?"

In a few words I told him of my toils and sorrows in the speech-making line, together with the devastating verdict of "Old Horace." I then requested that he hear my speech and give me his candid opinion of the whole matter. After I had finished the reading, he suggested only one change. In a number of places, I had spoken of the "Southland" for the "South." "Just leave off the 'land,'" said he, "and say the 'South.' Go back to your room and learn that speech until you can say it backwards, and you will win the medal!"

Walking on air with my head amid the stars, I went to my room.

At last the day came. We had drawn straws for position on the team, and I had drawn number four. While I was describing the poverty and ruin that had come upon the land and the people of the South at the close of the Civil War, I noticed that Colonel Killebrew of Tennessee, one of the judges of the contest, was weeping. He had graduated from the University before the war and had come back for a reunion of his ex-Confederate comrades. Seeing his emotional reaction to my speech did not discourage me as to the final outcome!

President Venable awarded the diplomas, announced the recipients of prizes and awards, and announced that the winner of the Mangum Medal for Oratory was—Charles E. Maddry!

I might say that "Old Horace" never mentioned the matter to me again.

III

Teaching and Preaching

I SOON FOUND my schedule for the fall term at the University difficult indeed. From my father's home the daily trip was six miles. After a few weeks, I realized that some other arrangement for room and board must be made. Home was overcrowded, and there were too many mouths to feed, especially in view of the fact that I was no longer working and contributing to the support of the family.

I arranged to cut firewood for a cousin for my room rent and boarded wherever I could find work or credit. I managed in various ways to get through the fall term but could see no hope of staying on for the spring session. At this critical juncture in my personal affairs, the committee of Strain's school district offered me the school for three months. They reported that the county appropriation for the year was $80, and they would give me the entire sum for teaching three months! I felt highly honored that I should be invited to teach my home school! The salary offered—well, it seemed princely to me.

Before giving the committee a final answer, I felt that I must go into town and talk the matter over with Mrs. Sallie May Wilson, a teacher in the Canada High School, where I had prepared for the University. On a Sunday night during the Christmas holidays of 1898, I went into town for the evening service at the Baptist Church, knowing I would find my teacher in her accustomed place in church. On the walk to the village, I planned and rehearsed my presentation of the crisis that had come into my life and my decision to leave school and give up the plan of trying to graduate. I had long dreamed of studying law and from childhood had felt a desire to get into politics. The $80 I would make teaching would pay my debts, buy me some clothes so sorely needed, and enable me to attend the summer session of law school. Another session of teaching would enable me to finish the law course and hang out my shingle at the county seat!

The plan was so perfect and the prospect so enticing that the walk of three miles to the village was over before I had fully built up every line of defense in my glittering plan. I walked home from church with Mrs. Wilson. Before the cozy fire in her little living room, I found it strangely difficult to unfold my far-reaching and ambitious plan. Before I proceeded very far, I found I had run up against a determined opposition that I had not anticipated and was unprepared to meet. As my devoted teacher argued, wept, entreated, and prayed, somehow the offer to teach the home school did not seem so flattering, and the life of a lawyer and politician lost much of its glamor. The question of the ministry was opened afresh, and to my great surprise she told me of her long-continued interest and increasing prayer that I might be divinely led in my final decision on this matter of supreme importance. Sometime toward midnight, after I had given my teacher my solemn promise that I would never leave the University without first coming to talk the whole matter over with her, I left.

The next day I sought out the school committee and informed them that I had decided to remain in the University. To my surprise and delight, they decided to defer the session until July the first and offered me the school. Without hesitation, I accepted this offer, and on January 1, 1899, I went back to my studies.

I began teaching my first public school at Strain's Schoolhouse, three miles northeast of Chapel Hill, on July 1. Some sixty pupils were enrolled, ranging in age from five to twenty-one. There were several grown boys enrolled with whom I had attended school at this same place. They were generally very co-operative and helpful.

On the first morning as school assembled, I was faced with the question of whether or not to read the Bible and pray. Most of the teachers who had gone before me would read something from the Psalms or Proverbs but would not have a prayer. I felt it was my duty to have both. There were present grown boys and girls with whom I had mingled in all the social contacts and activities of the neighborhood. To stand before this group and read the Scriptures and lead in prayer was a major effort to one who suffered acutely from self-consciousness. However, I have always been glad that I followed my better judgment and opened that first day with divine worship.

This session went smoothly and was a moderate success; the patrons were pleased, and everybody was happy. I learned more than my pupils did and have always been grateful to a kind Providence that I had this valuable experience that so richly influenced my life.

Early in September the school closed with a rather pretentious "exhibition." On the closing night when the committee came in a group and formally offered me the school for the next summer, I accepted and thus insured the improvement of my financial situation and the completion of my course in the University.

The second session seemed to give general satisfaction. I left the old community with regret, yet with a feeling of pride that I had taught in the old log house where my father went to school in his boyhood and where he taught in his young manhood. Here in the same hallowed spot, I had learned valuable lessons in the long process of getting an education—a process that was then just beginning.

I first saw the North Carolina Baptist Convention in action in the fall of 1900 when it met in the First Baptist Church of Raleigh. It proved to be a historic session. I was a junior at the University and went as a messenger from the Chapel Hill Baptist Church.

Since this was my first attendance at the meeting of a state convention, I was tremendously impressed with the proceedings. For the first time, I saw the leaders among the Baptists of the state, laymen and preachers. I heard N. B. Broughton, F. B. Hobgood, and John A. Oates, along with other prominent laymen, little dreaming that one day I would be Mr. Broughton's pastor. In a rough and tumble debate on the *Biblical Recorder*, I heard the young and brilliant editor, Josiah William Bailey, speak. He clashed with N. B. Broughton, and before the debate was over, Baylus Cade and J. D. Hufham were drawn into the fray. It was a battle royal when these two stalwarts contended.

One other incident in this, my first convention stands out as vividly in memory after the passing of fifty years as if it had been yesterday. Secretary John E. White resigned to accept the pastorate of the Second Baptist Church of Atlanta, Georgia. His resignation was accepted, and a large committee was appointed to nominate a new secretary. The committee brought in the name of Livingston Johnson, pastor of the First Church of Greensboro. After he was elected with unanimity and enthusiasm, President Marsh invited the new secretary to come to the platform to be presented to the convention. Secretary Johnson expressed his deep appreciation for the confidence the convention had reposed in him in a few well-chosen words, and he earnestly entreated all the messengers to pray for him that he might always be faithful to the trust they had just committed to him. Someone then suggested that the convention engage in prayer for the new secretary. The further suggestion was made that all who could possibly do so kneel on the pulpit platform around the newly-elected secretary, and that the dearly beloved and saintly Henry N. Brown, pastor of the First Church, Winston, lead the prayer. This was all done in a spirit of quiet and holy reverence.

It would have seemed wholly beyond the realm of possibility and entirely in the region of fantasy if anyone had suggested that just twenty years from that day I would be called to this office of secretary of the convention by the unanimous vote of my brethren.

In June, 1901, the YMCA Conference of the colleges and universities of the South met for ten days at Bingham Heights, Asheville, North Carolina. The University YMCA sent Louis Round Wilson, S. M. McNeely, J. M. Justice, and Charles E. Maddry as delegates. It was a memorable gathering of the religious leaders of southern schools. Here I heard the outstanding leaders and preachers of the Protestant churches of America. My spiritual life was greatly enriched, and my vision of world Christianity was much enlarged.

The Southern Baptist Convention met in Asheville in May, 1902. I was pastor of five small churches which paid a combined salary of $430 a year. Tobacco being the main money crop in this section, most of my salary was paid in the fall. I wanted very much to go to the convention, but lacking the necessary funds, I gave up the cherished dream of seeing this great meeting.

Less than a month before the convention, to my surprise, a committee from my field of churches notified me that they were making up a purse to defray my expenses to Asheville. This good news brought much joy to my heart, and I immediately began to prepare for the memorable trip. In due time, the committee presented me with a purse of some eighteen dollars for the expenses of the journey.

When I boarded the train in Hillsboro, I met for the first time Reverend Hight C Moore, pastor of our church at New Bern. Already he was widely known through the *Biblical Recorder* as a gifted writer on Sunday school and scriptural topics. Mr. Moore informed me that he had engaged a room in a private home in Asheville and would be glad to share it with me. Thus began a lifelong friendship with Dr. Moore that has grown closer and more precious through the years. Four years after that first meeting, in the little church in Hillsboro, he performed the marriage ceremony which bound me in wedlock to his wife's first cousin. Some years later he assisted in the marriage ceremony of our daughter in his home in Nashville.

Charles E. Maddry while Secretary
of the Foreign Mission Board, 1934

Charles E. Maddry
at seventeen

Charles E. Maddry at Southern
Baptist Theological Seminary, 1906

The sight of so many Baptists in one meeting, and especially the presence of so many preachers, left an indelible impression on my mind. A local paper said there were fifteen hundred ministers who attended the convention. Up to that time it had not occurred to me that there were so many Baptist preachers in the world!

For me, the crowning thrill of the convention was the matchless sermon of Dr. George W. Truett at the First Baptist Church on Sunday morning. I had attended a conference on evangelism earlier, and when I reached the First Baptist Church at 10:45, every seat was taken, and the building was filled to the doors. The usher said that the only seat available was on the pulpit steps among the palms and flowers. I took the seat offered and looked at the mighty preacher through an opening in the palms.

Dr. Truett at this time was only thirty-five years of age, but already his fame as an eloquent preacher had penetrated to every state and community within the bounds of the Southern Baptist Convention. It was indeed a thrilling and momentous hour, and the great man was at his best. It was his first appearance as a preacher before the people of his native state, and hundreds of them packed the large church to hear him. Some dozen years before this time, as an ambitious young mountain boy from Clay County, he had passed through Asheville on his way to seek wider fields of opportunity in great Texas. He had now come back to his native hills, already famous throughout the nation as an eloquent minister of the gospel.

In the evening, at one of the smaller churches, I heard the renowned Texan, B. H. Carroll, for the first and only time. Those who were competent to judge in such matters reported that it was a deep and learned doctrinal discourse. Attending so many sessions of the convention throughout the week, together with the emotional upsurge of the Truett meeting at the Sunday morning hour, had left me with little enthusiasm for anything but sleep. After seeing that the great Carroll was safely launched on his hour and a quarter discourse, I promptly went to sleep!

In the early days, Baptist churches, in voicing their approval of a candidate for the ministry, always spoke of the matter officially as "liberating the young man to exercise his gifts in the ministry." Later, if the candidate proved himself worthy and demonstrated to the church and the public generally that he possessed gifts commensurate with the high calling to which he aspired, he was ordained.

All through the years of my boyhood and young manhood, I heard much of a divine call to the ministry. Often the preachers I knew discoursed from the pulpit on the necessity for an unmistakable, heavenly call. There was held up before us the call of the Old Testament heroes and prophets—Abraham, Jacob, Moses, and Isaiah. As we were led through the New Testament, we saw clearly the divine hand and heard the irresistible voice calling John the Baptist, the apostles, Barnabas, and Saul. Especially was great stress laid upon the conversion and call of Saul of Tarsus.

From the time I professed Christ and joined the church at eleven until I was twenty-four years of age I was greatly concerned, and at times deeply troubled, over the question of what I should do in life. I held such an idealistic and lofty conception of the ministry that I did not feel that I could ever be worthy to enter upon the duties of such a sacred calling. When I compared my experience with that of ministers whom I heard relate their experiences, I *knew* I had not been called to the responsibilities of such a high and holy office.

One incident in my boyhood exerted a great influence upon the decisions of those early days, as well as upon the conduct of all of my later life. I am not sure of the time, but I think it must have been soon after I joined the church, that Mother told me how before I was born, she had prayed and yearned for her third child to be a boy and for God to make him a preacher. At that time, she was not openly a professing Christian or a member of the church. I remember distinctly, although I was only about five years of age, Mother making a profession of faith in Christ at a revival meeting at Old Orange Methodist Church. She had put the younger children, including myself, on a quilt under the bench; I remember being awakened by the shouts of the people, seeing the sputtering tallow candles with which the church was lighted, and hearing the people say that my mother had been converted. My judgment after all the years is that Mother was at the time already a believer in Christ, but that she had never openly confessed her faith until that night.

When I started to high school in the fall of 1896, the old longing to be a preacher came over me afresh, but I kept the matter locked in my own heart and never breathed to anyone the turmoil and unrest of my soul over the momentous question of my life's calling and responsibility.

Finally, I mustered up sufficient courage to talk the matter over with my pastor, the Reverend J. F. Duffie. Sympathetic and helpful, he insisted that I allow him to take the matter to the church, asking that I be "liberated to exercise my gifts in the ministry." I was very skeptical of possessing any "gifts" in the direction indicated. Being afflicted with a terrible sense of unworthiness, self-consciousness, and timidity, I refused for several months to consent to the matter being brought to the attention of the church.

During the annual revival, as the service was closing one afternoon, the pastor, without consulting me, announced that the church would meet the next morning at ten o'clock for a prayer meeting and added, "Brother Charlie Maddry will lead." This announcement threw me into a dither of nervous excitement and dread! What was I to say next morning? I had never attempted to speak in church, and the very thought of such an undertaking left me in a panic. On reaching home, I took my Bible and went off to the woods, where I stretched out on the pine needles under a great tree. I spent two hours praying as best I knew how for divine help for the ordeal of the next morning. My mind finally settled on the Isaiah 55. I spent the hours until twilight, meditating on this great Scripture and praying for guidance in this crucial hour.

It seemed to me that everyone was present the next morning—kinfolks, playmates, stern deacons, critical old ladies in split bonnets, and members of the gang of gay young swains with whom I had engaged in the semi-forbidden things upon which the church frowned.

My first attempt to lead a church was not, to say the least, a glowing success. It wound up in an emotional breakdown. After the pastor led a closing prayer, I slipped out a side door of the church to seek composure and solitude in the woods adjoining the church grove. The devil came in a terrific onslaught saying: "That was a ridiculous spectacle you made of yourself, and you thought you were called to preach! I would never try again!" I went home in the depths of despair. My disappointment and sense of frustration and defeat can only be understood by one who has undergone a like experience.

Some two years passed, and I was nearly half-way through my sophomore year at the University. On the first Sunday in December, 1899, Father came by the school and took me with him to the Saturday meeting at Mt. Moriah Church. The pastor preached; then he called the church together into conference. After all the business for the month was finished, the pastor came back into the congregation where I was sitting and said to me, "What have you decided to do about this matter of surrendering your life to Christ for the ministry?" When I replied that I had been unable to reach any decision in the matter, he said that he was going to request the church to license me to preach. At once I was in a panic of fear and indecision. Although I begged him not to mention the matter to the church because of my uncertainty, he went back to the pulpit and stated to the church, in substance, that God had called Charlie Maddry to preach, but that he had been fighting the call for years. He recommended that the church set its seal of approval upon the young man by "liberating him to exercise his gifts as a candidate for the ministry." Some brother made a motion that this be done; the motion received a second and the pastor announced that the matter was open for discussion. There was a painful pause, and at last elderly Deacon Nash Cheek, himself a licensed preacher, rose to say that he thought highly of the young man, that he had known his grandfather and father before him. He said he had no objection to "liberating" the young man but that he had never heard him preach and did not know whether he had any gifts for the ministry. He suggested, therefore, that the motion be laid on the table for the present and that an appointment be made for the young man to preach some Sunday afternoon in the near future, after which the church could decide the question upon its merits.

Thinking the time had now come for me to speak, I arose to remind the church that I had not requested the action contemplated. I reminded them further that granting me license to preach would not make me a preacher unless God had called me, and that withholding such action would *not* keep me from being a preacher if this was God's plan for my life. I added that I had no intention of preaching a "sample" sermon; and moreover, I had several years ahead of me in the University and seminary if I should decide to preach. After making it plain that I was not seeking the action contemplated by the church, I left the matter in their hands. There was further discussion, the pastor urging favorable action. Finally Brother Cheek graciously withdrew his objection, and Mt. Moriah Church "liberated" me to exercise my "gifts as a candidate for the ministry." One more step was taken toward my becoming a preacher.

Most of the Negroes with whom I grew up in the Presswood Creek community were members of Mount Sinai Baptist Church, located some five miles away on New Hope Creek. Since there was preaching only once each month at Sinai, the Negroes of the local community conducted a Sunday school at Rosemary, their district schoolhouse, which adjoined my father's farm. Shortly after Mount Moriah granted me license to preach, Rosemary friends sent one of their leaders, a life-long friend, to search me out at the University for the purpose of expressing to me their unbounded joy over the good news that I had decided to enter the ministry. They also expressed the sincere hope that I would honor the Rosemary congregation with my first effort to preach the gospel. This friend assured me that they were all "hongry" to hear me, and I accepted their invitation, setting an early date for my visit.

On the appointed day, with joy in my heart that the Lord had provided one congregation who believed in me and wanted to hear me try to preach, I made my way three miles over the hills to my old home on Presswood Creek. I looked forward with keen delight to the privilege of speaking to those friends who were always sympathetic and responsive. Then this thought came to trouble me: suppose the news had gone abroad that I was to make my first effort to preach that day and the kinspeople and neighbors, other than my colored friends, should be present to hear me! I knew that my style would be decidedly cramped if my fear proved correct.

I reached home in this troubled state of mind, and found Mother in the kitchen preparing dinner. Upon my asking the whereabouts of Father, she said that he was in the "big house" dressing to go with me to Rosemary. I told her that I was badly scared already and that I certainly would be in a nervous dither if Father attended the service. She said she would try to persuade him not to go. In a short time, she returned to say that, while he was keenly disappointed, he would forego the pleasure of hearing my first attempt to preach.

The congregation was out in full force. The older men and women present had been born in slavery and knew the bitterness of human bondage. They had gone through the terrible days of Reconstruction and the never-to-be-forgotten terrors of the Ku Klux Klan. Several of them were Baptist deacons, and the majority owned their own farms.

They gave me a warm and enthusiastic welcome. The presiding officer conducted the service with dignity and dispatch. The congregation sang several spirituals that had been favorites of mine from childhood. An opportunity was then given for all to speak who desired to do so. Most of the older heads spoke words of appreciation and good wishes for the young visitor.

About twelve o'clock, all minds being at ease, I was presented to the congregation by the chairman. He reminded the congregation that my grandfather, Captain Abel Maddry, had been the unfailing friend of their fathers during the bitter days of slavery, and that he had championed their rights in the old days before the war when the black "servants" were members of Mount Moriah Church along with the white "masters." He recalled the service Grandfather had rendered the newly-freed black people in 1868 when, as chairman of the committee from Mount Moriah Church, he had led in the organization of Mount Sinai Church. He further reminded his audience of the never-failing friendship of my father for them through all the years since the home-going of my grandfather.

After expressing my sincere gratitude that these friends of all the years since childhood had been the first to invite me to speak to them in my new role as a candidate for the ministry, I reminded them that I was not yet a preacher and that long years of toil and study lay ahead before I would be prepared for the work of a full-fledged minister.

I then read the tenth verse of the fourth chapter of Zechariah: "For who hath despised the day of small things." I simply pointed out the way in which Divine Providence had seemed to lead me since childhood. I drew the conclusion that it all clearly indicated that my desire and purpose to become a minister had the approval of the Great Head of the Church. I closed with an earnest appeal that these early and devoted friends bear me up continuously in their prayers, asking that God would make me humble and worthy preacher of the gospel of Jesus Christ. The service closed with many devout "amens."

Thirty-two years after, I was formally invited to come back to Rosemary for the anniversary of that first sermon. There were five present who had heard me on the former visit, and one brother even remembered the text. The singing was glorious, and all present had a joyous time.

In the old days before the Chapel Hill Baptist Church was organized, the Baptists of the University village affiliated with the Mount Carmel Church, located four miles south of Chapel Hill. Dr. William Hooper, noted scholar and teacher, minister of the Episcopal Church and professor at the University, was baptized into the fellowship of Mount Carmel Church by Reverend Patrick W. Dowd in 1831. He later became president of Wake Forest College.

On Friday evening before the first Sunday in June, 1900, Reverend W. D. Bostick sought me out at the University and said that he was called away for a funeral and wanted me to preach for him at Mount Carmel Sunday morning. I tried in every way to get out of the assignment, but the pastor said that he had tried every possibility and that I was his last hope. I finally consented to go. He informed me that Professor J. W. Gore, who was a member of the church at Mount Carmel, would lend me his horse and two-seated phaeton for the trip. The congregation was small. The sermon was noted neither for substance or homiletic merit, but I did the best I could. The people were appreciative and considerate.

On the first Sunday in July, the pastor was again called away and sent me in his place. Perhaps I did a little better on this second trip. After the service was over, a small group of men gathered about me in the church yard. One of the leading members of the church, a man who was reputed to be "well fixed" in material things, said, "Brethren, this young man has supplied our pulpit for two months. We ought not to allow him to go away without paying him a small sum, anyway."

Reaching into his pocket, he brought out a long, rusty-looking leather bag of a purse, snapped it open, fished among the bills and silver dollars, and brought forth a quarter of a dollar. Holding out his hand to the half-dozen men in the circle, he said, "Come on, brethren. Let's give the young brother at least a small token of our appreciation."

The men began to feel in their pockets and search their clothes, but little was forthcoming. I never heard of so many men in one group who said they had changed clothes that morning and left their purses at home! Finally, one brother found ten cents and another found a nickel. The prominent brother presented me with forty cents and expressed his regret that the offering was not larger. I protested that I did not expect anything, but I accepted the gift. It was the first money I ever received for preaching—forty cents for two sermons! I went on my way certain that I had been overpaid.

During the two years of my stay in the University, I was actively affiliated with the Baptist church of the village. I attended Sunday school and prayer meeting and sang in the choir. The pastor at this time was the noted ex-Confederate chaplain and "unreconstructed rebel," Dr. J. William Jones of Virginia.

In July, 1901, just after I had been elected County Superintendent of Schools, the pastor, who was going on his vacation, invited me to supply the pulpit for two Sunday mornings during his absence. Dr. Jones said that my many friends in the village were eager to hear me preach and insisted that I give them this opportunity.

I had known everybody in the community from childhood. Many relatives were in the town and surrounding country. I had spent two years in high school with the children and young people of the village. To the business people and housewives I was plain "Charlie Maddry," the awkward, overgrown country boy who sold produce and firewood to the folk of the town. Now it was rumored that I had been "called" to preach and was going to make my first appearance in the new role at the Baptist church the next Sunday morning.

During the week I suffered much doubt as to what I should say in my first sermon to my home folk. I remembered what Jesus had said about the honor of a prophet among his people and in his own house. I prayed much and prepared the best I could.

The little church was filled. It seemed to me that everybody was there. The University summer school students, mainly schoolteachers, came out in considerable numbers; several members of the faculty were present. I was scared and embarrassed, but whatever I may have lacked in polish and scriptural insight was counterbalanced by simple, unpretentious earnestness. The friends were kind and appreciative. One more great hurdle had been surmounted in my struggle to become a minister; I had faced the dreaded ordeal of preaching before my home folks and had found it not so bad! The pastor came back and, to my surprise, gave me a check for ten dollars—five dollars each for two sermons! I felt he had paid me far too much!

Sometime later, in the absence of the pastor, I preached at night. After service, I was escorting a young lady home, and we were walking some fifteen feet behind one of the deacons. It was dark and the street was unlighted. I heard the wife of the deacon say, "What did you think of the sermon?" The deacon replied, "Well, the young brother covered all the territory from Genesis to Revelation."

The county town of Hillsboro played an important role in my life. It had been laid out in 1754 and from the very beginning had been a center of culture and political influence in the life of the state. The Regulator trouble and the tragedy of Alamance had centered in this western outpost. The first open struggle of the oppressed masses in America for freedom from British tyranny and oppression had had its center in the frontier country town. Hillsboro was the capital of the state during the latter years of the Revolution. Here Cornwallis made his headquarters after the costly battle at Guilford Court House. Here, in 1788, the famous Constitutional Convention, after many weeks of bitter debate, rejected the Federal Constitution by one hundred votes. Through all the years down to the present day, Hillsboro has been the home of many leaders in the life of the state and the nation—governors, United States senators, Supreme Court judges, and others prominent in various phases of the life of North Carolina and the Union.

In the years before the Civil War and for two decades after the surrender, the Baptists had flourished and played a worthy part in the religious life of the community. However, in the closing years of the nineteenth century, the Baptist church had lost in membership and declined in strength until in 1901 there were just twenty-one members. An absentee pastor came only once a month to preach at the morning and night services. The salary paid was seventy-five dollars a year, and the rent of the small parsonage constituted the major portion of this amount.

I was invited to supply the pulpit on the fourth Sunday in July, 1901. After accepting the invitation, I hired a horse and buggy from a livery stable and drove the twelve miles from Chapel Hill on Sunday morning. When I arrived at the church, there were two young ladies sitting on the steps. One of them, whom I had met some months before at a picnic, introduced me to her friend who was the church organist. Five years later, I married the church organist whom I met that morning.

Since there was no preaching in the town on this day except at the Episcopal church, the congregations from the Baptist, Methodist, and Presbyterian churches were out in full force. They had heard of the young student who had dared oppose and defeat the long-time county superintendent of schools, and they filled the Baptist Church to see what he could do in the preaching line. It was a trying hour for the young minister. Just before I read my text, a deacon came to the pulpit and asked me to announce preaching for eight o'clock that evening. To my inquiry as to who would preach, he replied, "You, of course." I protested that I must return to Chapel Hill that afternoon, since I had hired a horse from the livery stable and had promised to return the rig before dark. Remaining deaf to all the appeals of the deacon to stay over and preach that night, I announced that there would be no evening service. I failed to tell the deacon and the congregation my real reason for not preaching at night. I had but one meager sermon, combined from the only two I had made up to that time!

Upon invitation of the church, I preached for them again the fourth Sunday morning in August. I spent the night at the hotel and paid the bill myself. I settled the livery stable bill incurred on the first trip as soon as I got my first pay as superintendent of schools.

The church forgot to pay me anything for these first efforts, but the Lord paid me most bountifully in giving me, out of the trip, the lovely and unsurpassed bride who has unfalteringly walked by my side for almost fifty years!

IV

Dedication and Preparation

In the spring of 1904, at the age of twenty-eight, I was compelled to face a new crisis in my lifework. For many years the conviction had been growing upon me that the Great Head of the Church had called me into the ministry. It gradually dawned upon me that I was making slow progress in entering fully and completely upon my lifework. I was a pastor—or more accurately, supply preacher—for four weak and undeveloped churches, with a total membership of less than two hundred and fifty, active and inactive. To these churches, scattered over the northern half of Orange County, I preached regularly eight times each month, thus being compelled to drive over a hundred miles every month, in all kinds of weather, over roads and trails that were all but impassable half the year round. Since I had not received any special training for the work of the ministry, patient and devoted country deacons taught me how to conduct a church conference, baptize believers, and administer the Lord's Supper. There was no special training for the young people in any of my churches, but a Sunday school of sorts was usually carried on from April until Christmas.

After three years with my field of churches, I realized that I was trying to do the work of two men in dividing myself between the county school work and the work of the churches. I realized that since I was not doing either job effectively, a choice must soon be made between the two. I wanted to preach, and I found the people eager to hear and responsive to the appeal of the gospel. Because there was little time for study, sermon preparation was made at night and during the long drives over the county. All in all, I felt a growing sense of dissatisfaction with existing conditions and knew that soon I would have to face the whole matter and make a decision that would affect, in a far-reaching way, all the years of my life.

Three years devoted to the work of public education in Orange

County had fully awakened me to the pitiable and desperate need for aggressive leadership in the schools of the county. All the progressive people had responded to my leadership by favoring a forward-looking program for better school buildings, better teaching, longer school terms, and more money for public education. When I came to cast up accounts, I was surprised and delighted with the progress we had made in so short a time. It all convinced me of the fact that the school work was a full-time job for a man trained in modern school methods. Since I had not had such training, I realized that sooner or later a trained educational person would be needed for the best interests of the children of the county. When I made known my purpose to spend some time in study at the Southern Baptist Theological Seminary, the Board of Education, voted to elect an acting superintendent, hoping that at the end of nine months I would return to my old job. With this in mind, my former pastor and devoted friend, Reverend John C. Hocutt, was elected acting superintendent.

The school people wanted me to stay; the dear people in the churches said that my preaching was good enough for them and urged me not to leave them. I remember saying to a saintly woman, who was insisting that all the people in the churches were satisfied with my preaching, that I was afraid that those coming on twenty years in the future would not be content with the ministry of an untrained preacher.

I sold my horse and buggy and settled all my affairs in Hillsboro and then went over to Chapel Hill to complete a transaction which brought great satisfaction to my heart. At various times during my years in the University, I had been compelled to borrow small sums from the Deems Fund—a loan fund established for the help of needy students. My total loans for the four years amounted to only one hundred and fifty dollars. At various times Horace Williams, Collier Cobb, S. M. Gattis, John T. Weaver, and Tom Strain had signed notes with me for these loans. I had promised them that the notes would be paid off at the earliest possible moment after I left school. I found that I could pay off all I owed in Orange County, including these loans from the University, and still have enough left to buy my ticket to Louisville. President Venable insisted that I would need the money for expenses in Louisville, and that the Deems Fund note could wait. However, I felt that I must keep faith with the men who had signed those notes with me. Therefore, I paid them off and left, completely free of debt. I set out, poor in this world's goods, but rich in faith that the generous Friend who had seen me through college would stand by me in my further efforts to prepare for my life's work.

On my last visit to Mars Hill Church, located three miles north of Hillsboro, I was surprised to see Mr. Edmund Strudwick and his young son come in as the service was beginning. He was a native of Hillsboro and a member of one of the most distinguished Presbyterian families in the county. He had risen rapidly in the business world, and was then president of the South Atlantic Life Insurance Company of Richmond, Virginia. He heard the announcements of the day concerning my departure in a few days for Louisville. I met him on the street the next morning, and to my surprise, he asked me if I had funds sufficient for my expenses while in the seminary. I replied that after all debts were paid, I had just enough for my expenses to Louisville. He inquired further as to how I expected to meet my obligations during my years of study in the seminary. I told him that I was going out in faith that work would open up and that I would find some way to finance the undertaking as the need arose from time to time.

Mr. Strudwick then said that he would like to invest something in my further training for the ministry. He gave me his address and instructed me to write him when I needed funds for current expenses while in the theological school. I borrowed small sums from him from time to time as the need arose, giving my notes to be repaid with interest. The total amount borrowed was $200. When I sent the first payment on the notes, I received a gracious letter from him saying that I need not send any further payments and that he was enclosing the cancelled notes. Thus God raised up an unexpected friend in another hour of need during my years of preparation for the work of the ministry.

Ever since that December day in 1900, when my home church at Mount Moriah set its seal of approval upon my life's purpose to become a minister, I had dreamed of the day when I could enter the Southern Baptist Theological Seminary at Louisville, Kentucky.

On the first day of October, 1904, along with some three hundred other students from widely scattered states and nations, I registered. I was tremendously impressed by the learning and ability of the faculty. It was a high privilege to sit at the feet of such men as E. Y. Mullins, A. T. Robertson, John R. Sampey, W. O. Carver, E. C. Dargan, and W. J. McGlothlin. Each was outstanding in his own field.

I still consider it one of the greatest blessings that ever came to me as an unworthy preacher of Christ's gospel—the high privilege of studying the Word of God for these months under the inspiration and guidance of such worthy and renowned teachers.

In the light of after years, I realize now more fully the value and worth of the fellowship and blessed associations formed during those crowded years of hard work at Louisville. Hidden from all human eyes at that time was the fact that the God of missions was preparing for a critical and testing time in the life of the Southern Baptists and their foreign mission work. A leader would be needed, together with a band of devoted men and women to support him and hold up his hands. Looking back now, I realize with humility and gratitude that all unknown to me or my associates, teachers and students, God was leading me on. In after years, many of these friends and fellow students of the Louisville years became staunch supporters and loyal helpers in the work of foreign missions, in state conventions, and in churches throughout the territory of the Southern Baptist Convention. Many of them, from time to time, were members of the Foreign Mission Board, state secretaries, editors of Baptist papers, pastors of loyal and devoted churches, and foreign missionaries.

Among those whom I knew in Louisville who, in later years, were to become pastors of great missionary churches were: J. Clyde Turner, A. Paul Bagby, W. F. Powell, C. B. Arendall, W. C. James, T. V. McCaul, W. C. Barrett, J. R. Jester, and W. O. Patterson.

Some of the candidates for service in the foreign mission fields, during those days of 1904-1906 were: J. H. Rowe, E. L. Morgan and wife, J. W. Shepard, Miss Cynthia Miller, Miss Alice Huey, Miss Rena Groover, C. K. Dozier, G. W. Bouldin, Dr. and Mrs. B. L. Lockett, H. H. Muirhead, O. P. Maddox and wife, Miss Maud Burke, Miss Sophia Lanneau, and W. W. Adams.

A few weeks after I entered the seminary, President Mullins sent for me to come to his office. He said the church at Mitchell, Indiana, had requested him to send them a preacher for the next Sunday and asked me to fill the engagement. I accepted the invitation and preached for the Mitchell church Sunday morning and night. They invited me back the next Sunday and in a few weeks offered to call me as pastor for full time. I soon realized, however, that my work in school was so heavy that it was not best for me to undertake to serve a church as full-time pastor.

In November, 1904, just after I declined the call at Mitchell, an opportunity to become pastor of a fine church in the Bluegrass section of Kentucky unexpectedly opened to me. One of the seniors, with whom I had become an intimate friend, came to my room with a letter from a deacon of the Evergreen Church at Farmdale, Kentucky, requesting him to send them a supply preacher for the next Sunday morning service. He offered me the opportunity to go, saying that they paid $15.00 for a supply for one service. I was eager to preach and needed the money! I accepted without hesitation.

I found that the Evergreen church, made up of some of the most loyal and devoted people I have ever known, was in a bad tangle over calling a pastor. For a generation they had always had a seminary student to serve them. After the church had heard two "candidates," one had been called by one majority. The losing side refused to make it unanimous. They were in a deadlock, with neither side willing to give in.

All of this was known to me before I preached Sunday morning. It so happened that both of the men were my good friends in the seminary. Since I had not come with an expectation of a "call," I preached the best I could, had a good Kentucky dinner, and went back to Louisville on Sunday evening, content with a fine day enjoyed with the saints at Evergreen.

Eight days later, I received a letter from the clerk saying that the church had held a special meeting on the Sunday following my visit, rescinded their former action, and called me unanimously as pastor for half-time at a salary of $25.00 per month. I accepted the call and spent fourteen months with this delightful church. Life-long friendships were formed here which have blessed and enriched all the later years of my ministry.

But the months were passing rapidly, and soon it was time to be thinking of calls to pastorates and permanent locations. My heart turned with poignant and ever-increasing longing toward North Carolina. A call to a church in any state would have been welcome, but a call from some North Carolina congregation would have been especially welcome and appealing.

In the early spring a letter came from a field of churches including Graham, Haw River, and Sweptsonville. The salary offered seemed princely—$800 per year and a home. I investigated, wrote letters of inquiry to the state secretary, prayed and waited. The weeks were slipping by, and there was no other call on the horizon. A lovely young lady was waiting for me down in the Tar Heel State, and a decision had to be made. Seemingly, all other doors were closed; Graham was open, and so the decision was made.

I wrote two letters that night, one to the Graham Committee informing them of my acceptance of their call, and the other to the young lady informing her of the momentous decision. We would be married in May and begin life's journey together in the parsonage in Graham.

It was late in the night when the decision was made and the letters written. On going out to drop the letters in the mail box in front of New York Hall, the student dormitory, I heard an inner voice, clear and unmistakable, which said: "It's all right to mail the letter to the 'young lady in waiting,' but the letter to the Graham committee can wait another day, at least." The inner voice was so unmistakable and clamorous that the letter to the church committee was left on my study table, while I went to bed with the conviction that the whole question of my future place of service was still far from being settled.

V

Return to North Carolina

LATE IN THE FALL of 1905, plans, long in the making, began to take shape for the organization of a new Baptist church near what was then the Normal and Industrial College in West Greensboro. The idea was born in the mind and heart of Dr. Livingston Johnson, former pastor of the First Baptist Church of Greensboro, who, in 1905, was Corresponding Secretary of the North Carolina State Convention. The active leaders in the movement were O. Joe Howard, O. W. Monroe, J. S. Moore, O. Shell, C. E. Horton, W. E. Harrison, and Dr. Henry W. Battle.

This group, working through Dr. Johnson, invited me to come and lead in this new undertaking. After much correspondence the offer was accepted, and in February, 1906, I began a ministry of three and one-half years in the Gate City. I was pastor of Southside, a small mission church in South Greensboro, for half the time. They paid $150 per year. The new mission in West Greensboro promised to pay $350 and the State Mission Board paid $500 per year for the work at the two mission points.

The work grew rapidly, and in a month it was clearly seen that it would be wise to organize a Baptist Church in West Greensboro. Accordingly, on Sunday, March 11, the new church was constituted with forty-two members.

The church grew so rapidly and the demand became so insistent for the full-time service of the pastor, that a church meeting was held on June 27, at which time I was unanimously called as pastor at a salary of $1,000 per year. A committee was appointed to confer with Southside Church, requesting that I be released from half-time service with them on November 1, so that all my time could be given to the rapidly growing new congregation. The Southside church relunctantly consented to the request, and I was released after a service of six months.

On May 2, 1906, I married Emma Parker, daughter of T. B. Parker and Penelope Alderman Parker, in the Baptist Church in Hillsboro. The ceremony was performed by Dr. Hight C Moore, a relative of the bride, and the pastor of the church, Reverend A. C. Hamby. Dr. W. F. Powell, a seminary classmate and for many years pastor of the First Baptist Church of Nashville, Tennessee, was best man.

We began keeping house in Greensboro on Rankin Street. The panic of 1907 hit us hard, and the banks issued script instead of money. On December 13, 1907, our daughter, Katharine, was born.

Some months later it seemed to me that I could leave the work at Forest Avenue without hindering the growth of the church. When an unexpected call came from the First Baptist Church, Statesville, I accepted. The church had but recently built and paid for a new building. While the auditorium was amply adequate for the something less than three hundred members, facilities were wholly inadequate for the growth and development of the Sunday school.

The Statesville church has sent out a noted group of preachers and missionaries during the three-quarters of a century since it began its existence in the Court House in this pedo-Baptist stronghold. Dr. J. Clyde Turner, who became one of North Carolina's most noted and dynamic Baptist preachers, pastor of the First Church, Greensboro for more than a generation, was saved, baptized, and licensed to preach in this church. His father, John C. Turner, was senior deacon during my pastorate with the church.

This church sent forth Mrs. Maud Burke Dozier as a missionary to Japan. Southern Baptists never sent out a more successful and Christlike missionary than this noble woman. Dr. Charles L. Leonard went out from this church to China. The church has always been missionary in its practice and outlook, and the missionary cause had a devoted and enthusiastic friend and a generous supporter in Miss Laura Lazenby and her noble brother, L. K. Lazenby. Miss Lazenby, a noted schoolteacher, was a woman of genuine culture who always put her church first. By dint of thrift and wise foresight, through a long life as a successful teacher, she accumulated a respectable estate. As the end drew near, she visited the Secretary of the Foreign Mission Board in Richmond and made all necessary legal arrangements for her entire estate to pass to the Foreign Mission Board at her death.

In the fall of 1911, the Tabernacle of Raleigh invited me to make them a visit. It was one of the largest churches in North Carolina.

Led by N. B. Broughton, the Sunday school for years had been one most advanced in the state in modern methods of teaching and evangelism. It seemed to offer an outstanding opportunity for a wider service in the ministry. However, because of a decided distaste for the practice of preaching "sample" sermons before a church that was looking for a pastor, I declined the invitation to visit the church for the purpose of exhibiting samples as a candidate for the vacant pulpit. On the Monday morning following, I received the following wire:

Raleigh, N. C. Nov. 1
Rev. Chas. E. Maddry
Statesville, N. C.

The Tabernacle Baptist Church of this city, in conference assembled tonight, extends unanimous call to you to become its pastor and prayer was made that the Lord should lead you to acceptance of same. Letter will follow.

N. B. BROUGHTON

I accepted the invitation and on the first Sunday in December, 1911, began work in Raleigh as pastor of the Tabernacle.

Needham B. Broughton was a remarkable man of many talents. Born in 1848, eleven years before the outbreak of the Civil War, he knew the poverty and hardship of that terrible struggle and the greater social and economic upheaval of the long drawn out years of reconstruction.

After coming to Raleigh in early manhood, with limited formal education and without the backing of men of wealth and influence, he made a commanding place for himself in the business and religious world that was unique and unsurpassed. He educated himself, and by dint of uprightness of character and industry, established a printing, engraving, and bookbinding establishment that has grown and expanded through more than three-quarters of a century, until today the firm of Edwards and Broughton has become one of the largest of its kind in the South and is a synonym for careful workmanship and honesty in the business world.

N. B. Broughton was a pioneer in modern Sunday school methods, and before the turn of the century he had made the Tabernacle Sunday school famous for its advanced methods of teaching, effective organization, and evangelism. Throngs of children and young people were drawn into the life of the church. The church was a center of evangelism, and the "Lord added to them day by day those who were being saved."

The Tabernacle Church has been a veritable beehive of activity in the discovery and training of leaders for church and Sunday school activities. More than a score of young ministers have gone out from this church. Among the many who have become widely known in the religious world was the gifted theological teacher, scholar, and author of theological works—Dr. James McKee Adams.

The four and one-half years at Tabernacle were fruitful in the service of Christ's gospel and at the same time were years filled with hard work and much travail of soul in trying to be a faithful minister. Substantial progress was made in all phases of the work. There were many organized classes which were great factors in the life of the church. They were evangelistic agencies and did much to boost the attendance at every service. R. N. Simms and his sister, Mrs. Moseley, organized the first Baraca Class in the state, and the class, still taught by Mr. Simms, has had an honorable and remarkable part in the life and work of the Tabernacle. Other influential classes, taught by Major J. J. Bernard, Miss Maud Reid, J. M. Broughton, Sr., and E. H. Broughton, have all been mighty forces in the life and growth of the Tabernacle.

But the pride of the Sunday school was the unique "Infant Class" taught for a half century by "Mr. Joe and Miss Ida" Weathers. They were remarkable teachers and boosters. Not having any children, they loved and adopted all the children within the circle of the Tabernacle influence and loved them as their very own. This class was the pet and pride of the Sunday school and church.

N. B. Broughton made much of special days and exalted the idea of organized classes. He was far ahead of his day in Sunday school methods but was slow to take up the idea of a graded Sunday school. When his nephew, J. M. Broughton, Jr., came back from Harvard with his law degree, N. B. Broughton was a sick man. Young Melville had taught school for some time and had also been acting county superintendent of schools for Wake County. He saw at once that the next forward step in growth was the grading of the Sunday school. He was made associate superintendent, and with the support of the pastor and many of the teachers, the Sunday school was graded.

To attract and hold the people, I saw that much time must be given to study and sermon preparation. The pastoral work of the church was heavy indeed. There were always the many sick to be visited and the poor to be cared for. There were few automobiles in Raleigh in those days, and certainly the pastor did not have one. The house-to-house visiting required much walking. There were many funerals to be conducted. The former members of the Tabernacle were scattered widely in other states. When sorrow and death came, it was frequently the Tabernacle that was called upon to minister in the last hours of distress and need. All together, the work of preaching, church administration, and pastoral duties made a heavy load for one man, though he was young and vigorous.

Moreover, the church did not provide any assistance, except in the music program. There was a large and splendid choir, directed by a trained and efficient leader, but the choir director and the organist were the only paid workers besides the pastor.

During the first two years with the church, I did the preaching in the annual spring revival meetings of 1912 and 1913. There were eighty-odd additions in each meeting. The whole church was organized as far as possible for these meetings. A great deal of visiting and personal work was done. The pastor, deacons, Sunday school teachers, and leaders of women's work went afield for the lost, and the results were highly satisfactory. I have found that it is always effective and profitable for the pastor to hold his own evangelistic meetings as often as possible.

In 1914, led by the pastor, Reverend Walter N. Johnson, the church at Wake Forest launched an enthusiastic effort to erect a church building on the campus. Since the organization of the church, the congregation had worshiped in the college chapel. The whole denomination was conscious of the need for a separate house of worship at the college. A convention committee was appointed to work with the local Wake Forest church committee in the endeavor to raise the money needed from the churches for the undertaking. I was made chairman of this committee. Brother Johnson was made chairman of the local church committee and we worked together in fullest sympathy and understanding for the success of the undertaking. The Wake Forest Church did its part nobly. The trustees of the college gave the site for the new church. When the enterprise was well begun, Chairman Johnson was taken ill, and the whole weight of leadership fell upon my shoulders. This extra work, in addition to the labors of a large and exacting pastorate, all but crushed me, but somehow the venture was carried through to the successful and triumphant conclusion. I wrote many hundreds of letters and traveled widely among the churches soliciting funds for the completion of the enterprise. The church was finished and paid for, and the long deferred dream of the Baptists of North Carolina was realized—a beautiful and well-appointed church house stood on the campus at Wake Forest.

Texas Calls

In the early spring of 1916 there came an invitation from the pulpit committee of the University Baptist Church of Austin, Texas, that I make them a visit looking to a call to the pastorate of their church. After some investigation and correspondence with friends in Texas, I decided not to make the visit. At Easter time, Mrs. R. H. Baker, a leading member of the Austin Church, who had been visiting her son in Philadelphia, spent Easter Sunday in Raleigh. With convincing enthusiasm she laid the appeal of the University Church on my heart in such a way that I could not get away from the impression that God was calling me to this hard but compelling task. The University of Texas was growing rapidly and with its wealth in oil lands was destined to be one of the richest schools in the land. The lands allocated by the state to the University were already becoming valuable.

Around the turn of the century, a faithful and devoted group of professors and a few leading citizens, led by Judge John C. Townes, Dean of the University Law School, had organized the University Church. They had bought a small chapel from the Presbyterians two and one-half blocks from the main entrance to the University. Here the little church, consisting of less than two hundred members, was worshiping when they invited me to be their pastor and lead in the effort to build a worthy church plant across from the campus. A splendid lot had been bought and paid for.

Looking back now after a third of a century, I can see clearly the human factors that led up to the decision to move to Texas. Without adequate assistance, the ever-increasing load of preaching and pastoral work incident to a large church in Raleigh was more than one man could successfully carry. The pastoral work alone was more than one man could do, since the membership was widely scattered over the city, and there was no way to reach it except by daily, continuous walking. I was forty years old and knew the time had come for harder and more systematic study of the Word of God if I was ever to attain to the dream of the years of becoming a good preacher. Through all the years, the growing passion for world missions had dominated my life. In this move into a new fellowship, I felt that God was leading me into greater open doors for world service.

VI

University Church, Austin, Texas

I REACHED Austin June 1, 1916, and was met at the train by Judge John C. Townes, Dean of the University Law School and chairman of the Board of Deacons of the University Church. He was a gentle, Christ-like man, loved and honored by everyone. After being entertained in his home for a few days, I secured a room at the Y. M. C. A. My wife and little girl stayed in Raleigh until early in September.

On the first Sunday in June, 1916, I preached my initial sermon before a congregation which filled the small chapel of the church. Dr. J. B. Gambrell, General Secretary of the Executive Board of the Baptist General Convention of Texas, came to be with me that day. He would not preach but consented to "greet" the people at the close of the service. It was a typical Gambrell deliverance, which delighted the people.

I had just gone through two years of intense and consuming effort as chairman of the convention committee trying to persuade the churches of North Carolina to build a worthy church and educational plant at Wake Forest. I realized at once that there was no commitment by the state board or denominational leaders of Texas of a definite amount which the denomination was willing to invest in a church plant near the University of Texas. I found also that the University Church, composed largely of professors, students, and people directly or indirectly connected with the University, had no practical conception of the cost of an adequate church plant for the spiritual welfare of the hundreds of Baptist students. I preached that June Sunday morning with a sense of humility and the utter need of divine help.

At the night service on this first Sunday in Austin, I baptized four fine students into the fellowship of the church. I soon saw that the work with students was vastly different from what I had been used to in former pastorates in North Carolina. This was more individual and took time and patience. The general evangelistic appeal from the pulpit had to be preceded by much personal work and teaching; the social contacts were highly valuable and fruitful.

I spent the summer months visiting and getting acquainted with the local membership of the church. It was hot, hard work walking over the white limestone streets and byways of North Austin trying to arouse and enlist the contingent of the congregation that was outside the University faculty-student group.

The latter part of August, before going back to North Carolina to bring my family out to Texas, I decided to make a trip to Dallas for a conference with Dr. Gambrell concerning the extent to which the State Mission Board was willing to help in financing the proposed new building.

Truly one of the greatest Baptist leaders of his generation, Dr. Gambrell was a man of the common people—simple, modest, unassuming. His manner before an audience was easy, and his speech was leisurely and understandable even to the most unlearned. Little children delighted to hear him, and, like his Lord, "the common people heard him gladly." His choice of simple Anglo-Saxon words was impressive, and no listener ever failed to understand his meaning. At times his audiences were moved from laughter to tears or to impressive silence. He was a combination of wit, humor, pathos, and simple greatness, all in one, often with each trait struggling for the mastery in the same breath.

Moreover, he had an imposing personality, with his fine physique, ruddy complexion, white hair, and white cropped beard. His dress was plain, at times almost to the point of shabbiness; his manners were simple and refined. He had been a famous Confederate captain under Lee and was one of his most dependable and trusted scouts. Even in age, he carried himself with an erectness and grace that singled him out in any gathering.

Such was the man that the Baptists of Texas and the South loved and delighted to honor. He was at various times editor of the Baptist Standard, state secretary of the Baptist General Convention of Texas, and president of the Southern Baptist Convention.

Therefore, it was with a sense of humility that I faced the great man across his desk on that August morning. I had come as a humble suppliant, seeking denominational funds for a needed and long-neglected state Baptist enterprise located at the main entrance of the fast-growing University of Texas. I knew that success or failure of the plans depended upon the work of this trusted and beloved leader of the Texas Baptist hosts. And now, at last, I was to hear in terms of dollars and cents to what extent the great leader was willing to commit the denomination to the long-dreamed-of undertaking.

Before getting down to business, we sparred with each other for some minutes over small and commonplace trivialities. Dr. Gambrell was completely at ease and busied himself, as he expatiated on the virtues of daily economy, by trimming his beard with the shears on his desk while explaining that he saved a barber's bill by trimming his own whiskers. I attempted to lead him back to the theme of the building of a worthy church plant near the University of Texas. This provoked a thirty-minute dissertation on the manner in which the great enterprise could be carried through to a successful conclusion if all concerned would do their best—the local church, the State Board, and the wealthy friends scattered over Texas. After reminding him that the local church had about exhausted itself in the purchase of the magnificent site, I tried repeatedly to pin him down to a definite statement as to the amount the State Board would give toward the undertaking. He continued to speak in expansive terms of how it would take patience, faith, and hard work to accomplish the undertaking. Since I was getting nowhere with abstract generalities, I boldly asked for a specific commitment from him, explaining that we could not employ an architect to design the building until we had this information.

Seeing that the time had come for a definite answer, the secretary replied that he had thought much about the matter, but that in the light of the mission resources in sight, he thought about ten thousand dollars would be the limit to which he felt the denomination should go in providing the "meeting house" needed by the University Church.

I confess that I was overwhelmed with amazement and despair. The walls of my dream house collapsed utterly, and I was speechless. I had expected not less than an initial gift of $50,000 and $50,000 more to be paid over a period of five years!

The interview closed, and I slipped away to catch a train. I am sure that the great man, with his irrepressible sense of hope and optimism, never knew of the bitter anguish and sorrow of soul with which I journeyed back to Austin that August night in 1916. There were no stars of hope shining for me as I drove by the newly-purchased site for the home of a greater University Baptist Church.

There was gloom in the University Church circles when I reported the outcome of my mission to Dallas. However, it did not last long. The little band of stalwarts in the faith of Christ and in the future greatness of their dream church soon rebounded to a sober and unfaltering faith that the glorious thing to which they had set their hands would one day be translated into reality.

In a few days I left for North Carolina to bring out my family. Henceforth we were to be Texans, and so far as I could see, our star of destiny hovered over the Lone Star State.

In the fall of 1916, the members of the University Baptist Church began with beautiful unity and contagious enthusiasm to plan for the construction of their sanctuary and educational plant. On the first Sunday in October, the student body came back, crowding the little chapel to capacity. I preached from Philippians 3: 13-14: "The Upward Calling of God in Christ." I had not planned to give an invitation for life service, but an inner voice whispered: "Give them an invitation for life service, and God shall lead." I gave the invitation. It was a tense and destiny-making time. Five students answered God's call with the surrender of life for service. Two of the young men became useful and successful ministers of the gospel, and beautiful brown-eyed Agnes Graham, a rising senior in the University, offered her life as God might lead for service on the foreign field. The congregation was stirred. It was a high hour and was but a prophecy of many holy and triumphant hours in the years that lay ahead.

Just as we were in the critical stage of our church building program, Jim Ferguson was elected governor. The University faculty and Board of Regents opposed him and his policies. In retaliation, supported by his followers in the legislature, he removed the Board of Regents, appointed a new group to do his bidding, and dismissed the president and many of the faculty. The move hit the University Baptist Church a stunning blow. Many of our leaders, deacons, Sunday school teachers, and prominent supporters, were dismissed abruptly without salary. Among those dismissed were Judge John C. Townes, chairman of our board of deacons, as well as several long-time professors. All of our plans were upset for the time, and a feeling of uncertainty settled down upon the church.

In a short time, however, there was a ground-swell of indignation that swept the state like a Texas tornado. The legislature, in special session, impeached the Governor and removed him from office. The Lieutenant Governor reappointed the former Board of Regents, who promptly restored the president and faculty to their former positions in the University.

All was again serene, and we took up anew our building plan for the church. It appeared for the time, at least, that our hindrances were over, and the future was rosy with promise.

The first great problem that tested the unity of the pastor and the people was the selection of an architect and the designing of the proposed building. One element of the church wanted a simple type of architecture with the main interest centered on utility and economy. The imperative need of the church was for ample auditorium space and adequate classroom space for the expanding Sunday school.

There was another element in the church consisting mainly of the group who were connected directly and indirectly with the University. This group, while not denying the need for economy and utility, were insistent upon the wisdom of expressing in wood and brick and stone the artistic and aesthetic religious appeal of a beautiful sanctuary. The lot purchased and paid for was ample.

The pastor earnestly desired a beautiful, artistic church building. At the same time, I was anxious to unite all of our friends behind the project—the local church, the State Board, and the friends, without going beyond the ability of the congregation to finance. To do this, it was felt that a practical southern-trained architect, who knew the requirements of an organized Sunday school, must be employed. The Sunday School Board's specialists were called in, and they rendered valuable service in planning a proposed educational building adequate for the immediate needs and the requirements for the foreseeable future. An architect employed widely by many prominent and growing Baptist churches throughout the South was called in. He studied the problem and produced a splendid layout for our needs as to space and modern educational requirements; but the external appearance of the building from the architectural and artistic standpoint was unacceptable to the committee. It was a splendid plan from the standpoint of utility and the traditional idea of what a Southern Baptist "meeting house" should look like, but the committee rejected the plan unanimously.

The building committee then began the search for another architect. Some of the members had seen the Pan-American Building in Washington, designed by Albert Kelsey of Philadelphia. The beauty and magnificence of it intrigued them. Correspondence was opened with Mr. Kelsey, and he was invited to visit Austin. He accepted the invitation and came. The committee was greatly pleased with his ideas and employed him forthwith to make preliminary studies of a sanctuary and educational layout in keeping with the surroundings and conforming to the general type of architecture prevailing in the university.

After a delay of some months, he came back for a second visit with the committee and submitted a plan that was beautiful and satisfying in every particular. It was to be a Spanish mission type structure with an imposing bell tower from which chimes could be heard all over Austin.

As to the cost of the church, the architect was vague. However, he had completely won over the committee to his viewpoint. He reminded them that the great churches and cathedrals of Europe were not built in a day and that the cost for a work of artistic beauty such as he had designed was a secondary consideration. The committee signed a contract with Mr. Kelsey.

I was keenly conscious through it all that an enormous sum of money was going to be required to finance such an undertaking. I knew also that fifty thousand dollars, payable through a period of five years would be all the local church, composed of teachers, small business men, and university students, could possibly give. The State Mission Board had indicated that ten thousand dollars would be about the share of the denomination at large. There was left that vague and uncertain amount expected from wealthy friends over the state. I knew a little of the cost of building in war times, and preliminary estimates ran all the way from three to five hundred thousand dollars. The committee, caught up in their artistic and aesthetic enthusiasm for the dream building of the Philadelphia artist, saw only the stars and knew it could be done. I knew that the best years of my swiftly passing life would be required to build and pay for such an undertaking.

In the midst of our preliminary preparation for raising all the money we could locally, the United States was drawn into the European conflict. President Wilson was re-elected with the slogan "He kept us out of war," and then the reckless and insatiable ambition of the German Kaiser drew America into the costly struggle. Our existence as a free nation was in the balance, and we went into the struggle with the firm determination to "win the war to end all wars."

Numbers of our young men both from the University and the local community went into the struggle at the beginning, and many of them never came back. All of our efforts and resources were invested in the all-out effort to win the war.

Just as we were planning to launch the educational unit of our church plant, a drought of unprecedented length and severity prostrated all farm and ranch activities in southwest and west Texas. The drought lasted for more than a year, and many thousand of cattle died for lack of grass and drinking water. Many ranchmen shipped their cattle to Louisiana to save the remnant. It was time of great distress, and the economic life of the whole southwest area was blighted.

In an effort to reduce the cost of the building, the committee at last faced the necessity of leaving off the proposed bell tower to the church. It was argued that this was to be separate and apart from the church; the bell tower could be added later when times were more propitious.

Just as I thought we were all set to let the contract for the educational wing, tentative bids revealed the fact that we lacked ten thousand dollars of having enough money in sight to pay for the proposed unit.

At this time, to complicate matters further, I received a letter from my life-long friend, Secretary of the Navy, Josephus Daniels, offering me an appointment in the Navy with the rank of Lieutenant-Commander, provided I could close up affairs in Austin immediately and go to France. The offer made a tremendous appeal to me, and I wanted very much to accept it.

A joint meeting of the building committee and the deacons was called, and the whole matter was laid before them. The discussion lasted until midnight. The pastor asked to be granted leave of absence for the duration of the war and that the building enterprise be postponed until after the close of the war. It developed that one member of the committee had challenged two friends, large cattlemen near Marfa in the Davis Mountains, West Texas, to give ten thousand dollars toward the finished structure. She had a feeling that if rightly approached they would give the amount for the educational wing.

Late at night, a motion was adopted instructing the pastor to make a visit to the good friends of the church and lay the whole matter before them. It was understood that if the effort failed, the building enterprise would be postponed for the duration of the war, and if it succeeded, the pastor would decline the offer of Mr. Daniels and remain with the church. I made the trip and was cordially received by Messrs. Bennett and Willis McCutcheon. The whole matter was canvassed with great care, and I was finally assured at the close of the second day's visit that the ten thousand dollars necessary for the completion of the proposed unit would be given, provided I would decline the proposal to go to France as a chaplain and remain with the church until the first unit of the structure was completed.

I returned to Austin, and we let the contract for the educational unit and the basement floor of the church.

We moved into the finished unit on November 10, 1918, and the Armistice was signed on the next day. I thus lost my chance to go to France, but the church secured the part of the building contemplated. I have realized long since that after much prayer and agony of soul God's plan was found, and His will was carried out.

In the meantime, even during the war years, the church was making satisfactory and commendable progress in every way. The congregations were growing, and the Sunday school was graded and standardized. The Student Department was organized, and the first Baptist Student Union in the South was constituted by O. P. Campbell, Secretary of Student Activities in the University Church, and J. P. Boone, State Baptist Young People's Secretary. The John C. Townes Bible Chair was organized under the tutorship of Mr. Campbell, and the University gave credits toward graduation for the work done in our church.

At the meeting of Baptist General Convention of Texas held in Waco in November, 1916, I was on the program to speak on evangelism. It was a high hour and gave me a splendid introduction to the Baptist hosts of the Lone-Star State. Following this, I was overwhelmed with invitations to hold evangelistic meetings in many churches throughout Texas. I held fruitful meetings with the First Baptist Churches in Tyler, Henderson, Corpus Christi, Gainesville, Texarkana, Baylor University and Mary Hardin-Baylor at Belton. I had good meetings also at Florence, Fort Davis, East Austin, South Austin, and the University Church. These meetings gave me wide contacts with Texas Baptist preachers and leaders. I made many friends for the University Church, and much later, in my years of critical service with the Foreign Board, Texas Baptists rallied around me in a loyal way in every hour of need.

After the war closed, the University Church made plans for the completion of the auditorium. We raised all we could locally and then secured a large long-time loan from a midwestern insurance company. The contract was let, and the work was begun in the last months of 1919. Progress was slow, materials were hard to get, and prices were high. The Texas Board made a substantial gift, and the Home Board made a loan that was later converted into a gift. The church was growing, and large numbers of the Baptist students in the University were continuously coming into the church.

After leaving North Carolina in 1916, I had severed most of my contacts with Baptist affairs in the home state. I had gone back for the commencement exercises at Wake Forest in June, 1917, upon the invitation of President Poteat and the Board of Trustees for the bestowal of the honorary degree of Doctor of Divinity. As time passed, the contacts with the Baptists in the home state gradually faded into the background, and I was becoming more identified with the Baptists of the Lone-Star State. I had been serving as a member of the Executive Board of the Baptist General Convention of Texas and was beginning to feel very much at home in the Southwest.

Baylor celebrated seventy-five years of glorious achievement in June, 1920, and conferred upon me the honorary degree of Doctor of Divinity.

The roof was going on the main church auditorium, and soon the building would be finished. I had purchased a home within one block of the church and it looked as if we were settled for life. My wife and my daughter were thoroughly identified with the people and were fast becoming loyal and enthusiastic Texans.

VII

Call and Commitment to Larger Responsibilities

In November, 1920, Walter N. Johnson, secretary of the North Carolina Baptist State Convention, announced his determination to retire from that position that he might return to the pastorate. Immediately there was intense interest as to who would be chosen as his successor. The convention met in Asheville, and when the call was made for nominations for secretary, some eight or ten men were nominated. On the first ballot, Charles E. Maddry was elected by a decided majority. The first news I had was the receipt of telegrams from various friends saying that I had been elected and urging me to accept.

I took the call of the North Carolina brethren as the call of the Lord. Amid sorrow and regret, I offered my resignation as pastor of the University Baptist Church, and we turned our faces toward our native state.

On January 1, 1921, I began the new work. My predecessor, Dr. Johnson, spent New Year's Day with me, introducing me to the work and doing all he could to help me get a comprehensive insight into all its phases. I soon realized that I had suddenly been thrust into the biggest and most demanding task I had ever undertaken. As the work grew in importance and the churches grew in numbers, the position of general secretary grew in responsibility.

The 75 Million Campaign had gone over in a great way in the churches of North Carolina. The same was true of every state in the South. The denomination, led by Dr. L. R. Scarborough, had gone all out to raise 75 million dollars for missions, with the pledges to be paid in five annual installments. The churches of the South had subscribed over ninety million dollars.

Knowing the problem among Southern Baptists of systematically

University Baptist Church, Austin, Texas

The Maddrys in Brazil in 1936 with Harley Smith,
Dr. and Mrs. W. B. Bagby, and Dr. and Mrs. L. R. Scarborough

The Maddrys and the J. B. Weatherspoons
at the grave of Henrietta Hall Shuck in Hong Kong

The Maddry Family: Mrs. R. W. Severance, (daughter Katharine),
Bob, Sarah, Dr. Maddry, Kay, R. W. Severance, and Mrs. Maddry

collecting pledges, I began immediately to organize the Baptists of North Carolina, association by association, for this purpose.

Early in March we began a series of associational rallies over the state. The heads of all departments went with me, and leading pastors were invited to assist in speechmaking. The new secretary thus had a good introduction to the pastors and representative men and women of the churches.

Much enthusiasm was manifested, and the meetings were well attended. Much lasting good came out of these rallies. At Statesville I was stricken with appendicitis and underwent an operation at Long's Sanatorium. My associates finished the tour in western North Carolina. I was out of the work for six weeks.

From early boyhood I had heard the people discuss the need for a new church plant adequate for the local congregation and for the Baptist students in the University at Chapel Hill. The little church building, erected in 1854, was located several blocks from the school. It was wholly inadequate and out-of-date. There was no provision for Sunday school or young people's work. In the fall of 1921 I assisted the pastor there in a gracious revival. Students and town people packed the little meetinghouse. There were a number of additions to the church. At the close of the meeting we raised more than ten thousand dollars for a new building. One member of the faculty at the University gave one thousand dollars, although he never attended the church. The secretary pledged substantial support from the State Board.

A serious problem soon threatened to dampen the ardor of many of the local congregation. The church had served the older families for seventy-five years. They were warmly attached to the old location. I frankly told them that the State Board would not be interested in building a new church on the old site.

We began at once the search for a new site nearer the University. After some months, we purchased a splendid lot at the corner of West Franklin and Columbia Streets, one block from the University. The old church property was sold, the proceeds going toward the cost of the new building. Later, when I presented the matter to the church, the vote was unanimous for moving to the new site.

The building of the Chapel Hill Church was but the beginning. The State Board took up with enthusiasm the plan to help provide a worthy and adequate Baptist church house at every school center. Some of the churches, such as Mars Hill, Chowan, and Wingate, had already begun building activities before I came to the secretaryship. In some cases their plans were enlarged, and in all cases the Board helped these churches pay off their indebtedness.

Secretary Livingston Johnson had launched the program of evangelism in a new and effective way. He employed two full-time evangelists, one for the east and one for the west. Dr. Walter Johnson continued this program, and I expanded and enlarged it.

North Carolina never had a more devoted denominational worker than E. L. Middleton. For many years he served as Sunday school secretary and led North Carolina Baptists to a high place in Sunday school work. He died in mid-life and left behind him a record for denominational loyalty and achievement in his chosen field.

Another worker who has won great renown in several fields of denominational activity is Perry Morgan. When I came to the secretaryship he was made state B. Y. P. U. secretary. He led the state to a worthy place in young people's work in the South. When E. L. Middleton was called home, Perry Morgan was elected Sunday school secretary. He carried forward the Sunday school work in a marvelous way. He left us to become manager of the Ridgecrest Assembly. Much of the advancement at Ridgecrest, especially in buildings and equipment, is due to the foresight and business ability of Perry Morgan.

Meredith College for women had long since outgrown the cramped campus in northeast Raleigh. It would cost more than a million dollars to secure a new location with ample room and to construct buildings sufficient to care for five hundred students. The denomination was unable to furnish the funds necessary to build and pay cash for the proposed plant. Finally the board of trustees, led by Gilbert T. Stephenson, business leader and banker of Raleigh, recommended to the convention that they proceed to secure a new site and issue a million dollars worth of bonds, underwritten by the state convention, for the purpose of building the new Meredith. The convention adopted the suggestion, and the bonds were sold. They were to be paid off in fifteen years out of funds given by the churches for Christian education. For two or three years the payments were met without much trouble. But as the depression of 1928–32 began to slow down the income from the churches, the Board found itself in financial straits and found it even more difficult to meet the payments on the bonds.

The convention had been organized at Greenville in 1830. I recommended to the session of 1927 that we plan for a worthy celebration of the centennial by raising a fund of a million dollars with which to pay off the Meredith bonds. The recommendation was adopted. The idea was received by the people in the churches with great enthusiasm.

Two years before the centennial we began the systematic organization of the associations for the campaign to pay off the debt on Meredith College. The plan was to organize the churches in every association for subscriptions from each church on a fixed date. All the forces of the convention were thrown into the movement—pastors, staff and departmental workers, college professors and students were enlisted in a united and determined effort to come to the centennial year completely out of debt. The secretary and the associate secretary, M. A. Huggins, led in the movement and traveled hundreds of miles over the state getting the organization set up. We made hundreds of speeches from Manteo to Murphy, and on the appointed day the pledges were taken in all the churches. More than eleven hundred thousand dollars were subscribed, the pledges to be paid in two years. We came back to Raleigh after six months of intense effort, feeling that the great task was accomplished.

In 1929 the financial panic was upon us. The churches were unable to pay their pledges and the convention was compelled to default on the payment of the bonds. Gloom and despair settled upon our Baptist people, and it was necessary to curtail the work of the Board in all phases. The high hopes with which we entered upon the work on January 1, 1921, were blighted, and we came to the centennial of the convention with a sense of frustration and defeat. The called meeting of the convention met at Greenville and bravely faced a gloomy future as we looked back on the triumphs of one hundred years.

I tried to put on a brave front and face the future with some degree of enthusiasm. Many of our churches had sold bonds to finance needed equipment for church and Sunday school enlargement, and many of them defaulted on the mortgage and bond payments. Pastors' salaries were reduced, and there was widespread suffering among all our people.

The one dominating motive that had influenced my decision to accept the call of North Carolina Baptists to come home and lead the missionary forces as general secretary of the convention at the close of 1920, was the missionary motive. I believed North Carolina Baptists were ready for a decided and enthusiastic advance in missions—state, southwide and worldwide. The conviction came to me slowly that my work was finished as general secretary, that the executive work of the convention should be in the hands of a younger man of business ability, and that I should devote the remaining years of my ministry to the work of the pastorate or to some phase of missionary promotion. In this frame of mind, I went to the annual meeting of the Southern Baptist Convention in St. Petersburg in May, 1932.

It was a time of financial distress and uncertainty for every convention, board, and educational institution among Southern Baptists. Dr. Fred F. Brown, pastor of the First Baptist Church in Knoxville, was elected president of the Convention. A brilliant and captivating preacher, his soul was aflame with missionary zeal and passion. His church was the largest weekly contributor to the Cooperative Program within the bounds of the Convention.

After much prayer and prolonged discussion, the Convention voted to organize and set up under the direction of the Executive Committee a new department, to be known as the "Missionary Promotion Committee." The duty of this new department was to press with renewed zeal and vigor a more generous and systematic support of the Cooperative Program, with especial emphasis on the tithe and on weekly offerings in the churches for the support of missions, benevolence, and Christian education.

One person from each state was appointed to organize and set up the new department, and I was appointed to represent North Carolina. The first duty of the committee was to elect an executive secretary for the new work of the Convention.

The committee met in Birmingham, Alabama, early in June. Two days and one night were spent in drawing up a statement to be sent forth to the denomination concerning the plans, purposes, and program for the guidance of this new phase of missionary promotion. When the details of this matter were finished to the satisfaction of the committee, the important question of the selection of a man to lead in this new and responsible phase of the Convention's work was taken up. After much prayer for divine guidance and much discussion of men and qualifications, a vote was taken, and Charles E. Maddry was the unanimous choice.

I came back to Raleigh, knowing full well that I had indeed come face to face with a decision that might well mean a complete and far-reaching change in all the course of my life. I faced the challenge of a new and untried work that would take me into all the states of the South. Some months before this, I had confided to my wife the fact of the growing conviction that my work was about finished in North Carolina. To my surprise, she quietly said that she had been praying about the matter for some time and felt that the time had come for a change in my lifework. In 1925, we had completed a new home in Raleigh and were well on the way toward paying for it. My wife's parents were living in Raleigh and were both beyond eighty years of age. We dreaded the thought of breaking all the ties that bound us to the Old North State and beginning all over again in a new community. However, we were to learn through the months and years that the work of the kingdom of God was not bound by state or national lines, but was as worldwide as man's sin and need for a Saviour.

It was a hard decision to make. I had enjoyed the confidence and loyalty of the brotherhood in North Carolina in a most remarkable and satisfying way for eleven and a half years. There was no division in the ranks, and so far as I could see, the happy relationship of loyalty and fellowship would have been continued.

After days of heart-searching prayer for divine guidance, I decided that God was leading in this new venture, and I accepted the work. A call for a special meeting of the general board was sent out for the latter part of June, 1932. I submitted my resignation effective July 15 and made preparation to move to Nashville, Tennessee.

Mr. M. A. Huggins was elected my successor, and for twenty-two years he has led North Carolina Baptists in a wise and constructive program. He is greatly beloved by all our people. It took him ten years to pay off the debt on Meredith College and redeem the honor and credit of the convention. He has served longer in the difficult and exacting position of general secretary than any other man in the more than one hundred and twenty years of the life of the convention.

Executive Secretary of Promotion–Southern Baptist Convention

On August, 1, 1932, I began work in Nashville as executive secretary of the Promotion Committee of the Southern Baptist Convention. I had an office with the Executive Committee in the Sunday School Board building. Walter M. Gilmore of North Carolina, who had worked with me as director of publicity for the North Carolina Baptist State Convention, was made publicity director for Southern Baptists. He was a tireless worker, and our close association in the denominational work bound us together in loving and helpful fellowship through the years.

The task to which I had been called was a new departure for Southern Baptists. It was an organized and aggressive effort to promote the Cooperative Program through stewardship, tithing, and the weekly offerings. The leaders were the state secretaries, pastors, and heads of all boards and agencies. The immediate objective of the Promotion Committee was to prepare the churches for a simultaneous every-member canvass in all the states during the month of November, 1932. The first task was the preparation of literature for this supreme effort in behalf of a united support for all our missionary, educational, and benevolent work through the Cooperative Program.

I left Secretary Gilmore to carry on the office end of the work in Nashville while I went afield, speaking before churches, associations, laymen's conventions and W. M. U. meetings in an effort to stir up interest and enthusiasm in a new and concerted movement for a more generous and united support of our work. I divided my time with the several state secretaries, who made the engagements and directed my efforts in the several states.

I filled engagements in Tennessee, Louisiana, Texas, New Mexico, Oklahoma, Maryland, and Virginia. The work was hard, the schedules were heavy, and long distances had to be traveled to meet engagements. While the progress toward a united program was encouraging, and the every-member canvass was a great advance over the old haphazard method of supporting the work of our Southwide boards, institutions, and agencies, it was far from being complete in all the churches. A good beginning had been made, but there must be more teaching and preaching of New Testament principles of stewardship before even a majority of the members in the thousands of Southern Baptist churches would come to a worthy and adequate support of all the missionary, benevolent, and educational causes embraced in the Cooperative Program. The way was opened for the larger enlistment in the co-operative work of Southern Baptists and the enlarged efficiency of the Executive Committee of the Southern Baptist Convention.

VIII

Accepting a World Commission

THE FOREIGN MISSION BOARD was in desperate financial straits. Not only had banks in Richmond refused further credit, but they were demanding substantial payments on their loans. Gifts from the churches were declining in an appalling way, and we faced disaster at home and abroad. The Board had made worldwide commitments for the support of American and native missionaries. These commitments could no longer be met, and the Board was facing the most embarrassing situation which had ever confronted it in the ninety-odd years since its organization in Augusta in 1830.

At the annual meeting in October, 1932, the missionaries on furlough, thirty-two in all, were instructed not to return to their fields, and the salaries, children's allowances, and house rent were discontinued. Some of these faithful servants of Christ were aged, sick, and suffering. Appropriations for native work, salaries of pastors, support of schools, hospitals, and all other phases of the work were drastically cut, and all work possible was discontinued at home and abroad. Many volunteers for world missions, already approved, were notified they could not be sent to their chosen fields.

The four banks in Richmond which held the Board's notes for one million dollars advised the Board that the total appropriation for the year 1933 must be held down to $600,000 and that out of this must be paid the interest on the loans. It was a critical hour for Southern Baptists.

The Foreign Mission Board had been looking for an Executive Secretary ever since Dr. Love's death. Dr. T. B. Ray, who had come to the Board in Dr. Willingham's day as Secretary of Education, had in turn served as Home Secretary and Foreign Secretary. In 1928, upon the death of Dr. Love, he had been made acting Executive Secretary, and in 1930, Executive Secretary. A committee which was appointed to seek for a permanent secretary had not been successful in finding the man they wanted who would undertake the heavy and responsible job of trying to save the work of the Board in the desperate situation confronting the Southern Baptist foreign mission work at that time.

Searching for a Leader

The first man approached was Dr. George W. Truett of Dallas, Texas. Dr. Truett declined, and the committee offered the position in turn to Dr. Fred F. Brown, Dr. J. B. Weatherspoon, Dr. Solon B. Cousins, Dr. Louie D. Newton, Dr. C. D. Daniel and possibly others. All declined. The Board met in annual session in October, 1932. After the committee had reported its inability to agree upon a man for Executive Secretary, the Board was then completely reorganized and L. Howard Jenkins, a prominent business man of Richmond, was elected president. A new committee on securing an Executive Secretary was appointed. They organized and evidently decided that the time had come to take a plunge, for the situation was desperate.

I had gone from Nashville to speak before the Knox County Baptist Association, meeting some fifteen miles from Knoxville. A messenger came out to the association with a request for me to call the Baptist Foreign Mission Board in Richmond. I was on the program to speak in the mid-afternoon.

After adjournment, I went back to Knoxville and put in a call for Richmond, but the connection was delayed, and I was just getting in bed at the hotel when the call came through. Drs. C. C. Coleman and John F. Vines informed me that the Board had just elected me as Executive Secretary and had adjourned after appointing them to notify me of the action. I was taken by surprise, because no member of the committee had ever approached me on the matter, but I informed the committee that the matter would be taken under advisement, and that they would receive an answer in a few days.

Certainly the leaders had taken a surprising and desperate gamble in calling me forth as the new Secretary. If I possessed any qualification for the position of leadership in the cause of foreign missions of Southern Baptists, it was my enthusiasm and my passion for world missions.

Before going to sleep that night in Knoxville, I called my wife and informed her of the surprising action of the Foreign Mission Board. Her reply was that she thought I had already a task in Nashville big enough for any one man.

On Monday, January 2, 1933, I entered upon my duties as the Executive Secretary of the Foreign Mission Board of the Southern Baptist Convention. The first secretary, Dr. James B. Taylor, a native of Britain, served twenty-seven years, from 1845 to 1872. Dr. H. A. Tupper of South Carolina served twenty-one years and four months, from 1872 to 1893. Dr. Robert J. Willingham of Georgia also served twenty-one years and four months, from 1893 to 1914. Dr. James F. Love of North Carolina served fourteen years, from 1914 to 1928. Dr. T. B. Ray of Kentucky served four years, from 1928 to 1932. I served twelve years, from 1933 to 1945. Thus these six men served the Foreign Mission Board as Secretaries for one hundred years.

A few weeks after I began my work in Richmond, a committee representing the four Richmond banks that held the notes of the Board for more than a million dollars requested Mr. L. Howard Jenkins, the newly-elected President of the Board, for a conference with chosen representatives from the banks. We went to see the bankers as requested. At the meeting of the Board on October 12, 1932, the budget for 1933 had been fixed at $600,000. Out of this was to come first the interest on our notes, amounting to $67,000. This left only $533,000 for all the work of the Board in 1933. At the October meeting it was found impossible to continue much of the work in foreign lands. When we met with the committee of bankers, we were informed that the Board must pay $150,000 of the $533,000 budget on the principal of the debt. My committee was thrown into consternation by this announcement. An earnest plea was made that the Board be allowed to go on with the budget as fixed in October. After quite a bit of discussion on both sides, Mr. Burnett, president of the First and Merchants Bank, who was presiding over the meeting, said that his committee would like to hear from the new Secretary as to his plans for paying the debts of the Board.

I then stated to the bankers that if they carried out their proposed plans to take out of our budget of $600,000, $67,000 for interest together with $150,000 additional to be applied on the principal of the debt, it would completely paralyze the Board as a going concern and bring disaster to all the foreign mission work of the Southern Baptist Convention. I reminded him that the Foreign Mission Board had been doing business with these banks for more than ninety years and that they had never lost a cent in principal or interest from our Board. I told them that Southern Baptists were going to continue doing foreign mission work and that if they persisted in their plans, they would put the Foreign Mission Board out of business completely. I also informed them that Southern Baptists would send their mission funds direct to the missionaries on the various fields over the world. I told them that our people would pay them every cent they owed them, providing they would allow us to carry on as a going concern. I further reminded them that their notes would be paid, every cent with interest, provided they allowed us to function as agreed upon at the October meeting of the Board. I stated that if they insisted on their demands as announced, their notes were not worth the paper they were written on and that they were planning to "kill the goose that laid the golden egg." Mr. Burnett said, with a smile, that that sounded like common sense to him. He asked for further discussion from his committee and they unanimously agreed to allow us to go on as planned at the October meeting of the Board.

The committee requested us to pay every cent possible if we should receive more than anticipated for the 1933 budget. We heartily agreed to this, and the meeting was adjourned with a feeling of confidence and a better understanding all around.

I will here anticipate events to say that in two years we had paid $250,000 on our notes. The crisis was past, and the credit of the Board was firmly established with the Richmond bankers.

The paralyzing debt began to bear heavily upon those who really loved foreign missions. It started first in Richmond. Dr. Wade H. Bryant, pastor of the Barton Heights Baptist Church, organized a club in his church with each member pledging to pay twenty-five cents a week for the debt on the Foreign Mission Board. Miss Blanche White, W. M. U. secretary of Virginia, heartily endorsed the movement and the W. M. U. organizations of Virginia took it up with enthusiasm. It spread rapidly among the churches of Virginia, and while it seemed small in the beginning, it was soon apparent that a similar method would eventually bring relief to the Foreign Mission Board if the other states of the South would take it up with the same enthusiasm. The Foreign Mission Board was able to report to the next Convention that several thousand dollars had been already paid on the debt.

At the meeting of the Convention in Washington, D. C., in May, 1933, the matter was brought before the people by Dr. Frank Tripp. A committee was appointed to work out a plan for the payment of the debts of all the boards, institutions, and agencies of the Convention. The committee reported a plan asking the churches to secure from every member as much as a dollar a month with which to pay all the debts of all the agencies of the Convention. Many church members took out several club memberships and thus the movement was an assured success. We owe an everlasting debt of gratitude to Brethren Bryant and Tripp for bringing forward a plan whereby the debts of the Convention were eventually all paid.

The Foreign Board in the flush days of 1920, out of receipts from the 75 Million Campaign, had purchased a wonderful piece of property, splendidly located in the heart of downtown Rome. In the summer of 1934, the Board sent the Executive Secretary to Rome to sell this property. The original cost was $180,000. After many difficulties, we sold the property to an international insurance company for $312,000. When the agent's fee, sale taxes, and other incidental expenses had been paid, I brought home and applied on the debts of the four banks in Richmond $292,000. The bankers were greatly pleased, and our credit was gilt-edged from that day. Within six months after we sold the property, Mussolini confiscated it for one-third of its value.

In the fall of 1933, in the midst of the worst financial storm America had ever experienced, at the annual meeting I presented to the Board a plan to provide for a modest pension for missionaries upon retirement at seventy years of age or upon becoming disabled by ill health before reaching the age of seventy.

The plan provided for the payment of five dollars by the Board and five dollars per month by the missionary. This was sixty dollars a year out of the meager salary of $800 per year paid the missionary. The Relief and Annuity Board was to handle the matter. The Foreign Board was the first Board or agency of the Convention to work out any plan of retirement for its employees. Dr. Thomas J. Watts was anxious to have our Board take the lead in the matter. In a few months all the other Boards and Agencies followed suit and the popularity of the Relief and Annuity Board was in the ascendency immediately. The missionaries henceforth upon retirement had five hundred dollars each per year. For a couple, that meant one thousand dollars per year. Many of them bought modest homes at our educational institutions and upon retirement settled in an environment where they were in touch with old friends and associates. The Board never did anything that was more popular and gave more satisfaction to Baptists in general. The matter took hold of me deeply because on the same day I was elected Executive Secretary thirty-two missionaries who were at home on furlough were dismissed. If friends, relatives, and churches had not come to their relief, they would have faced dire sufferings. I went over the South literally begging money for these stranded missionaries. I determined that such a tragedy in the lives of worthy and devoted missionaries and their children should never happen again.

For many years the Home and Foreign Boards had published a monthly missionary magazine called *Home and Foreign Fields.* The Sunday School Board paid for the publication. They lost money on the magazine every year. In 1937, the Sunday School Board reported to the Southern Baptist Convention that they had lost fifteen thousand dollars in the fifteen years in the publication of *Home and Foreign Fields.* They asked to be relieved of the burden.

This left the two mission boards without an organ of communication with the churches. I felt that something must be done to relieve this situation. I made a trip to Atlanta for a conference with Dr. Lawrence, Secretary of the Home Board. I proposed that we publish jointly a magazine edited by the Secretaries and paid for by the two boards. Dr. Lawrence replied that he preferred to publish a large home mission tract quarterly, and he did not believe we could succeed any better than the Sunday School Board had done with a joint magazine.

The Foreign Board had published a magazine just before the Civil War called *The Commission.* I decided to revive this magazine and called to my assistance Miss Inabelle Coleman, assistant to Dr. J. Clyde Turner in the work of the First Baptist Church in Greensboro. Miss Coleman had decided gifts as a writer and was a real artist in the make-up of the magazine. We proposed to publish four numbers the first year. The response was so generous on the part of the denomination that we published six numbers the first year. The price was fifty cents a year, and the subscriptions rolled in in great numbers. Some of my brethren said we could never publish a worthy mission journal for the ridiculous price of fifty cents a year. The magazine grew by leaps and justified my contention that with mass circulation we would make good. I edited the magazine for five years; then Dr. E. C. Routh was called as editor. He was a gifted and experienced editor and soon doubled the subscription list of the *Commission.* He was followed by Dr. Joseph Nordenhaug, who edited the magazine for some two years and then resigned to become president of our European Theological Seminary at Zurich, Switzerland.

He was followed by Dr. Frank K. Means. He is a gifted writer and editor. With the coming of World War II, the price of the magazine had to be increased to one dollar per year. The subscription list of *The Commission* had grown to more than one hundred thousand. The growth and popularity of the magazine has entirely justified the belief that an informative magazine at a popular price would appeal to the denomination. I sincerely believe that *The Commission* has played a major role in the rehabilitation of the work of the Foreign Mission Board at home and abroad. *The Commission* will compare favorably in literary value and influence with any denominational missionary journal published in America. Miss Marjorie Moore (now Mrs. O. K. Armstrong), Miss Ione Gray, and others have made it a very attractive magazine.

I realized early in my service with the Board that the work was worldwide in its ramifications and that one man alone could never meet the responsibilities and direct the operations of five hundred missionaries widely separated in sixteen different countries on three continents. In addition to the supervision of the work abroad, there was the conduct of the work in the homeland. When I went to Richmond in 1933, the staff consisted of the Secretary, one assistant secretary, the treasurer, one girl assistant, two stenographers, one woman who handled the distribution of study books, tracts and literature, and an office boy. This meant that there were eight persons in all to handle the Foreign Mission enterprise of six million Baptists gathered in seven thousand churches. It was an impossible situation, and before I had been in the work three months I determined to do something about it.

On my visit to Japan and China in 1935, I was accompanied by my wife and Dr. and Mrs. J. B. Weatherspoon. The Weatherspoons paid their own expenses, and I borrowed the money and paid Mrs. Maddry's expenses as I did on each mission tour. I had already made up my mind to recommend to the Board on my return the election of a regional secretary for the Orient. The question was upon the selection of the right man. Dr. Weatherspoon and I agreed that he should be an experienced man from China. I was seriously considering a brother who possessed many of the qualifications I felt were needed in this man. Dr. Weatherspoon advised me to wait until we reached Canton and see Missionary M. T. Rankin before making a decision. He had been a missionary in South China for twenty years, was widely known in mission circles throughout China, and was greatly beloved by missionaries and national Christians alike. For some years he had been president of the Graves Theological Seminary in Canton. He had married Valleria Greene, a daughter of Dr. George Greene, a North Carolinian and a missionary beloved in China.

We landed in Hong Kong one day about noon and met Dr. Rankin. Missionary John Lake had chartered a small steamer to carry our party to Tai Kam Island, ninety miles out in the China Sea, for a visit to his leper colony. He was to organize a church composed of forty lepers together with himself and wife. It was a great experience for all of us. About thirty Chinese leaders of the South China Baptist Convention together with quite a number of missionaries accompanied us.

On the way back from Tai Kam the next afternoon, Dr. Weatherspoon and I drew Dr. Rankin aside and sat down together in a little lifeboat. There, as our ship plowed its way through the quiet waters of the China Sea, we laid before Dr. Rankin our plans for the reorganization of our foreign mission work in the Orient and offered him the position. He was greatly surprised and could not give his answer at once. Some three weeks later, after he had prayed the matter through, he notified us that he would accept the call of the Board as the call of God. We had cabled our recommendation to the Board in Richmond and in a few days received a cable in reply saying that Dr. Rankin had been elected regional secretary for the Orient. I felt then, and I know now, that this was the greatest thing I ever did for foreign missions.

As I visited the other mission fields in Europe, Africa, the Near East, and Latin America, I recommended the election of regional secretaries for these areas. My recommendations were accepted by the Board, and George W. Sadler who had served many years as a missionary in Nigeria was elected for Europe, Africa, and the Near East, and W. C. Taylor was elected for Latin America. Dr. Taylor was succeeded by Everett Gill, Jr. Winston Crawley succeeded Dr. Gill.

IX

Visiting Mission Fields in Europe

EARLY IN JUNE, 1934, I started on my first visit to the European mission fields of our Foreign Mission Board. The purpose of this visit was manifold. First, the work in all the European countries, especially in Italy, needed to be reorganized and to have its relation toward the parent body in America reaffirmed. In the early days, the work, pastoral as well as church buildings and equipment, was supported by the Board in Richmond. There had been a growing feeling on the part of the supporting churches in the South and the Board in Richmond that the time had fully come for the national churches in the several lands in Europe to assume a larger share in the support of their own pastors and in the organization of new work in the regions still unevangelized in their respective fields.

After the Board sent the first missionary couple to Italy in 1872, the work was difficult and the progress disappointingly slow. The churches seemed content to continue receiving support from the Richmond Board and were doing little toward self-support. They were making little effort to evangelize the villages and towns in the outlying areas.

What was true of the churches in Italy was equally true in Spain, Jugoslavia, Rumania, and Hungary, for which Southern Baptists assumed responsibility after World War I. The new Executive Secretary was sent over by the Board with instructions to do everything possible to reorganize the work and to induce the churches to launch a worthy program of self-support and make an honest effort toward evangelism and expansion.

Our work in Europe was largely with the middle and lower classes. The economic status of the church members was very low, and the problem of making a living was vital. The work had always been generously supported by the friends in America, and the average church member was content to continue enjoying the bounty of their good brethren. It was easy for the pastors, who received a monthly check from Richmond, to make little or no effort to teach stewardship and self-support in the churches. If a new chapel or school was needed, generous friends in America would provide the money necessary.

Mission churches in other lands had this same attitude toward the question of self-support. I had found that true in the work of state missions in the home land. Churches that had been supported by the Board for a generation were sometimes reluctant to undertake self-support.

Accompanied by Mrs. Maddry, I sailed on a mono-class boat from Norfolk, Virginia. During the ten days of crossing, I had time for quiet rest and relaxation; I had little time for rest in the next three months.

After landing at Le Havre, France, we took the boat train up to Paris. We spent several days in Paris and made a brief visit to the battlefields of northern France. I was saddened and deeply impressed with the quiet and beauty of the Memorial Cemetery and battlefield of Belleau Wood. Here under neat marble crosses sleep more than 2,200 American men. All over Europe I saw these well-kept American cemeteries where lie buried hundreds of American boys who died in the vain belief that they were fighting to make the world safe for democracy.

From Paris we traveled to Madrid, Spain, where we were met by our missionary superintendent for Spain, Nils Bengtson.

English and Swedish Baptists were in Spain before World War I, but both of these groups retired after the war, and we assumed full responsibility in 1922 in accordance with the agreement in the London Baptist Conference in 1920. All Swedish Baptist missionaries in Spain had died or resigned except Reverend Nils Bengtson and his wife, faithful and worthy missionaries of this Board for many years.

The work has been slow and very difficult in Spain, which has been dominated by the Roman Catholic Church for centuries. The Reformation took hold of the upper and educated classes; they were the only ones who could read and thus learn the doctrines of Luther and Calvin. The Roman Catholic priesthood held the masses in ignorance and bondage to the Catholic Church. Since the Jesuits organized the Spanish Inquisition to root out the very seeds of the Reformation, Spain had suffered stagnation and death under the heels of Rome for three hundred years. Visitors are shown a public square in Madrid where 3300 martyrs to the cause of Christ and the Reformation paid the supreme price for their faith by being burned at the stake. Since the very seeds of Protestantism were rooted out, it can readily be understood why the soil of Spain has not been very fertile for Baptists and the Baptist message.

But in these years we have made a splendid and inspiring beginning.[1] Let it be remembered that the Baptist movement in Spain, as well as in all Europe, is a peasant movement, and while our people in all these lands are very poor, there is a vigor and virility about the work that promises much for the future. The pastors are, for the most part, untrained, but they are a devoted and courageous set of men. In a land of ignorance, superstition, arrested development, and stagnation, such as we cannot even imagine in America, they are bearing faithful witness to the gospel of Jesus as Baptists understand it.

We spent ten strenuous days with our churches in Spain and went on to Italy. In Genoa, we were met by our superintendent of the Italian Mission, Dr. D. G. Whittinghill. Ascending the imposing marble stairs leading to the magnificent station, I saw an elderly gentleman standing at the top of the stairway fanning himself with a straw hat. I drew near and said, "I am looking for Dr. D. G. Whittinghill, an American." He replied, "I am looking for Dr. and Mrs. Charles E. Maddry, of Richmond." Thus began an intimate and delightful fellowship with Dr. and Mrs. Whittinghill.

Some eighty years ago, Dr. George B. Taylor of Virginia, our first Southern Baptist missionary sent out from the homeland, laid the foundations for our work in Italy. In 1880 Dr. John H. Eager was appointed and labored for fifteen years. Fifty years ago the Board sent out Dr. D. G. Whittinghill to open a seminary for the training of a native ministry. After marrying Susy, the daughter of Dr. Taylor, he succeeded Dr. Taylor as superintendent and treasurer of our Italian Mission. Dr. Whittinghill did a far-reaching and monumental work in the training of a devoted and aggressive group of Baptist pastors and leaders. Almost every pastor we met in Italy had studied under him at some time. Mrs. Whittinghill was the founder of the Italian Woman's Missionary Union. Rev. J. P. Stuart and family and Rev. and Mrs. C. J. F. Anderson rendered short but fruitful ministry in Italy.

In 1904 Dr. Everett Gill, Sr., went to Europe and through the

[1] In 1953, 27 churches, 22 pastors, and 1804 members were reported.

years that followed did a notable work not only in Italy but the Balkans. He was our Southern Baptist representative in Europe 1921–1939. The Board never had a finer, or more gifted and capable representative anywhere than Everett Gill. He was always the patient, sympathetic gentleman; and Southern Baptists and the Foreign Mission Board owe him a debt they can never pay, for the discreet and Christlike way in which he administered our work in Europe and the Near East in those critical and trying years following World War I. Mrs. Gill was equally efficient and helpful in leadership among the women. She and Dr. Gill both have made a lasting contribution to our Baptist work in Europe by writing and preparing mission study books and literature for the missionary societies, churches, training schools, and theological seminaries. Loved and honored by all who know them, the Gills are now retired and live in Wake Forest.

Faithful Italian preachers, grounded in the doctrines of the New Testament, have valiantly preached the Word and spread the good news through the years. Many of these devoted servants of Christ have suffered for the sake of the gospel; many have been relentlessly and cruelly persecuted by Rome and her blind and fanatical priesthood, and even today they themselves, their wives, and their children, suffer in untold ways for the sake of the gospel.

Everywhere I went in Italy, I found the people hungry for the Bread of life. The people came in crowds to jam the churches and preaching halls to hear sermons preached stumblingly through an interpreter. And everywhere there were confessions for Christ—in some places faster than they could be counted. It is significant that most of those confessing Christ were adults. In their conservatism and reaction against Rome's method of receiving children, perhaps our pastors have gone too far the other way in their reluctance to insist upon young people coming to Christ. The churches were failing in the teaching and training of their young people.

For years Baptist pastors and churches in Italy were not taught the vital importance of becoming self-supporting and independent, but they are not to blame for this situation. The idea of an independent, self-governing, self-supporting church, made up solely of baptized believers, maintaining and supporting their own work and worship, gained headway slowly.

After visiting many of our churches, from the valleys of the Alps on the French border in the north, to Naples in the south, I called a meeting of all our station pastors in the city of Rome, on July 22,

23, and 24. They were all there, and it was the first time in eight years they had been together for a general meeting of any kind. Some of the pastors had not seen each other for over ten years. I had drawn up beforehand and had translated into Italian a suggested plan for the organization of a National Italian Baptist Union and a mission board. This plan, which we submitted on the first day of the meeting, provoked a three-day debate.

The following is a brief summary of the plan of organization suggested:

Believing that the time has fully come when the Italian Baptist Mission should assume more responsibility for the financial support and direction of our Baptist work in Italy, and believing that Baptist churches should at the earliest possible time become autonomous, self-governing, self-supporting, and self-perpetuating, we, the representatives of the Foreign Mission Board of Richmond, Virginia (U.S.A.), offer the following suggestions, looking forward toward the reorganization of our Italian Baptist Mission:

An Italian Baptist Union shall be organized. The *object* and *purpose* of the Union shall be,

(1) To elicit, combine, and organize the strength, energy, and zeal of Italian Baptists, for the purpose of carrying out the great Commission of Jesus to give the good news of salvation to all the world, beginning in Italy; to teach and train disciples in all the things commanded by Jesus and to do all other things possible to hasten the Reign of our Blessed Redeemer on earth, as we may be led by the Holy Spirit.

(2) Every organized church shall be entitled to send TWO messengers to the annual meeting of the National Union and ONE additional messenger for every unit of twenty-five members after the first twenty-five.

The item that caused so much debate was as follows:

(6) The Board of Directors shall take out articles of incorporation under the laws of Italy and shall take and hold title to all property hereafter acquired by the National Union, such as chapels, preaching halls, pastors' houses, and all other property that may be used for purposes of worship in the conduct of the general work of the Union. The Board of Directors shall be the legal and responsible entity for the conduct and direction of all Baptist work in Italy; it being the purpose of the Foreign Mission Board to turn over to Italian Baptists the church buildings now used strictly for worship and as homes for pastors; it being agreed that no property given by the Foreign Mission Board shall be sold or mortgaged without consent and approval of the Foreign Mission Board.

This was finally adopted when the Foreign Secretary announced that the American Board would withdraw from Italy unless the plan submitted was adopted. The Italian pastors voted with great reluctance to accept it.

When we took over the work of English Baptists in Italy in 1922, we bought their chapels and pastors' homes. All this property cost us a "pretty sum," and we owed for it in the banks of Richmond. In addition, we bought some thirty-five acres on a hill overlooking the city of Rome, and in the heart of the city we bought a whole city block. However, the government had declared this property to be within the zone of "monuments of antiquity," and we could not change the property, improve it, sell it, or build upon it, without the consent of the government. After eighteen months, some twenty acres of our suburban property were expropriated by the government for a gymnasium for their Balilla, or young people's movement. We did everything possible to secure payment for this land; the United States Embassy did all they could to help us. We did finally get the government to fix a price for the land taken—one third of its assured value, and they promised to pay us lira 951,000 ($82,000), setting the date for payment as July 28. Later they promised to pay us lira 500,000 on September 28, and the remainder the next July. Later they expropriated the remainder of the suburban land and finally, after long delay, the government paid for it at their own valuation.

At this time negotiations were begun to sell the downtown property, the results of which enabled us to apply $292,000 on the debt of the Foreign Mission Board.

Accompanied by Dr. Whittinghill, we called upon the brilliant and influential Italian attorney of our Board, Mr. Del Fratte. This gentleman was highly considered in international legal circles and enjoyed a large and lucrative practice. He was the legal representative for the United States Government in the delicate and tedious negotiations leading up to the purchase of the magnificent Embassy building in Rome, located a short distance from our property on Piazza Barberini.

Mr. Del Fratte was a freethinker. He had married a charming American Presbyterian woman who was a particular friend of the Whittinghills, the leaders of our Italian Mission. Through this social connection, our Board was able, for twenty-five years, to command the services of this leading attorney for a nominal annual retainer.

Mr. Del Fratte received us with all the grace and charm of a polished and cultured Italian gentleman. After a few minutes of polite conversation, we proceeded to the business in hand.

"Mr. Del Fratte," said Dr. Whittinghill, "Dr. Maddry is the Executive Secretary of the Foreign Mission Board in Richmond. He is here under instructions from his Board to negotiate a sale of the Board's Piazza Barberini property. He wants to employ you to handle the whole matter for the owners in America."

"Yes," I said, "The Board has at last fully decided to sell this property just as soon as a purchaser can be found. We have become alarmed after our recent experience with the high-handed and unjust methods of the Italian government in the Monte Mario property transaction. I am here under instructions to arrange for the sale."

"Have you been able to secure the approval of the leaders of the Italian Convention for this sale?" asked Mr. Del Fratte. "I am informed that they have taken the position that this property was purchased as an intended gift for the work of the Italian National Baptist Convention. They feel that the proceeds of this sale should be used in Italy for the enlargement of the Italian work. Unless they are satisfied and approve the transaction, your efforts to sell the property are doomed to failure."

"We have been in session with the leaders of the Baptist work in Italy for four days. Last night a compromise was unanimously agreed upon, and as you can see by this resolution, this phase of the matter has been settled in a way satisfactory to all concerned."

Mr. Del Fratte carefully examined the paper presented to him. "It is fortunate, indeed, that you have first arrived at a satisfactory understanding with your co-religionists here in Italy. Their approval and co-operation are necessary."

"Do you think you can sell the property? How much can you get for it?" inquired the debt-conscious mission secretary.

"The property," replied Mr. Del Fratte, "is easily worth half a million dollars. It we were given a free hand in an open market, it would bring that sum. But I am reliably informed that Mussolini has already decided to expropriate this property for his new building for the Department of Foreign Affairs of the Italian Government. Orders have gone forth for the preparation of architectural plans for the building. He is only waiting for the furor created in Washington over the Monte Mario steal to die down before proceeding with this new seizure.

"My advice to you is to make a sale as soon as possible." The attorney continued, "Italy is already bankrupt. Mussolini is seeking for new sources of taxation. If he does not confiscate your property straight out, he will levy a heavy capital tax that will consume it all anyway. You are both heretics and foreigners in Italy. My advice, therefore, is to sell at once and sell only for dollars, American exchange in New York. If you sell for lires, you will never be able to get a penny of the money out of Italy."

"Well, Mr. Attorney, the matter is in your hands. Proceed as soon as possible to find a purchaser who has sufficient financial backing in New York."

"I have a good prospect already, I think. An international insurance company with plenty of financial backing has decided to establish an European headquarters, and they are giving Rome first consideration. I have a 'hunch' as you Americans say, that I have a good chance to make a sale to them."

After the final details of our business matters were settled, Mr. Del Fratte invited the Americans to dinner the following evening. He had a magnificent estate, a beautiful villa located on four acres of land on the crest of Monte Mario, overlooking the Vatican and the "City of the Seven Hills."

After dinner, our host grew communicative and talked of Italy and her coming doom under the domination of the "Sawdust Caesar."

"Tell us, Mr. Del Fratte," said the Mission Secretary, "With your well-known and outspoken views on democracy and the freedom of the individual, how have you escaped the wrath of the Fascist Dictator all these years?"

"Well," replied Mr. Del Fratte, "Thereby hangs a tale. Many years ago, my father who was a prominent attorney, a freethinker, and a passionate advocate of the freedoms of the mind and conscience of the individual in all matters of religious faith and civic conduct, clashed with the authorities in Rome. He was thrown into prison and refused a hearing on the trumped-up charges filed against him. In spite of all his efforts to have the issue brought to trial, he languished in prison for several weeks. He was finally released, the charges against him having been dismissed. He came out of prison embittered against the ruling powers."

"So I judge you hold the same views of your father concerning civic and religious liberty."

"Yes, I am a firm advocate of civil and religious freedom for every soul in the world. We have little of either in Italy. I hate Mussolini and all his works. He is fast leading Italy to a doom worse than that visited upon her by the Goths and Vandals in the fifth century. I see nothing but ruin awaiting my country and my people. The end is not far away. The crash is on the way, and it is going to be appalling when it comes."

Six months later, in mid-Pacific on a ship bound for the Orient, I received from Rome a long radiogram in code, which when translated brought the thrilling news that the Piazza Barberini property had been sold for $312,500 payable in American dollars in New York!

The Mission Board's credit was saved. The faith and morale of the denomination was lifted to new heights. For once the "Sawdust Caesar" had been outwitted.

The property in Italy had been a hindrance and not a help to us. It took much of the time and energy of one missionary to look after the property and collect the rents. In addition it had created a false impression upon our Italian brethren because it led them to believe that we were rolling in wealth and would continue to support them forever. Therefore, this property was harmful, not beneficial, to our Italian work.

After our work was finished in Italy, we left by train for Oberammergau, Germany, to see the Passion Play. We were assigned to the home of the man who played the part of Christ. To be in this delightful home was a distinct privilege. We met interesting people and enjoyed our stay there.

The play itself is indescribable. For eight hours, along with four thousand other guests from all over the world, I was enraptured and enthralled with this incomparable drama which is put on every ten years by these simple peasants of the mountain village of Oberammergau.

We spent ten days in Berlin attending the meeting of the Baptist World Alliance. During our stay in Germany, President Hindenburg died, and Hitler came to power. It was an exciting and crucial time for the German people.

I had been invited to deliver an address before the World Alliance, the subject assigned being "The Implication and Outreach of the Great Commission." The addresses were printed in German, and all were carefully censored by the German committee. All references to democracy were carefully eliminated.

In 1921, as a result of the decisions of the London conference, the Foreign Mission Board had begun its work in Hungary in co-operation with the Hungarian Baptist Union. The close of the first World War had left the people of Hungary in a tragic and deplorable plight. Never in modern times has a people been more terribly punished for a losing war than Hungary was at the Paris Peace Conference. By this treaty, Hungary lost seventy-one per cent of her territory and sixty-three per cent of her population. It was hard for a great modern nation like Hungary to live under the conditions imposed by the treaty. A great French geographer has declared that the territory of Hungary before the war was the "most perfect geographical unit in the world." Hungary had possessed everything a modern nation needs to make her great—mountains, waterpower, coal, iron and other minerals, forests, building stone, navigable rivers, and a vast and fertile plain, which has been called the "granary of Europe." At the close of World War I, Hungary had 23,000 Baptists, organized in an efficient and progressive union. The division of Hungary left the Union with 7000 members.

Our Baptist work was prosperous, considering the conditions existing in Hungary. We owned the seminary buildings, the gift of Miss Varina Brown of South Carolina. This property, formerly a magnificent home, was located on a very prominent boulevard across the Danube from the great Parliament buildings. It extended through the block facing on two streets. In this property were several stores and apartments, which were rented.[2]

The territory of Jugoslavia lies along the Adriatic Sea, from Trieste on the north to Albania and Greece on the south, and inland to the Danube River. The name means "South Slavs," and the people belong to the great Slavic family. Intensely religious and musical, they are an aggressive, vigorous, hardy, and virile race, constituting some of the finest raw material in all Europe from which to make Baptists. They live in the very region adjoining Macedonia where Paul preached and established churches nineteen hundred years ago.

The story of the beginnings of our Baptist work in Jugoslavia sounds like a second record of the Acts of the Apostles being written today. The work had its beginnings in 1922. Though the population is made up of many language and dialect groups, the people are all cousins and of one Slavic origin.

The supreme need was for someone to teach and train a native ministry. God had called and raised up a worthy and promising group of young men for the ministry, but they were helpless without someone to teach and guide them.

Rumania is made up of many different nationalities and language groups. Our Baptist people there were divided into four language groups; and there were four Baptist Conventions, dividing the people according to differences of language—Rumanian, Hungarian, Russian,

---

[2] Since World War II and the inclusion of Hungary and contiguous nations in the Soviet orbit, we have little information concerning Baptists in that area. We do know that God is still at work behind the Iron Curtain.

and German. Because the Rumanian Convention had been torn asunder by strife and discord, there were two conventions of the Rumanian language group.

The fact that our Baptist movement all over Europe was a peasant movement will explain many seeming contradictions one found in our work in most countries. For unnumbered centuries, the peasant had been oppressed and ground down by both the state and the church, either Roman or Greek. For generations he had been kicked around as the underdog. Then a New Testament was put in his hands, and he was taught to read it. A Baptist missionary came along and preached to him that all men are equal in Christ, that in a Baptist church *everybody is somebody* in Christ. The new wine of spiritual freedom and equality went to his head, but there were others in the church with the same ideas. The result was a contest for leadership, and the biggest man won out and tried to lord it over his brethren, somewhat like the priest once did over him and his fathers. So it was only natural and human that these contests arose to trouble a growing spiritual democracy that had not yet become intelligent and capable of governing itself. This explains much of our trouble in many mission fields.

In 1934, Southern Baptists had work at only two places in Syria—at Beirut, the growing and expanding French seaport, and at Kefr Mishky, a Syrian village in the interior valley between the Lebanon and Anti-Lebanon Mountains.

S. M. Jureidini, a native of Lebanon, Syria, attended the 1893 World's Fair in Chicago. He was converted, joined the Third Baptist Church, St. Louis, and was baptized by Dr. W. R. L. Smith. In 1895 he opened work at Beirut where he labored for years. He and other workers were supported precariously by groups of American Baptists until after World War I, when Southern Baptists entered Syria and Palestine in the early '20's.

The work at Nazareth was begun years ago by Brother and Mrs. Mosa, and later his nephew, L. V. Hanna and his wife assisted them. For a while the work seemed to prosper, and the little church grew in a very encouraging way. I suppose Nazareth was selected for reasons of sentiment. However, Nazareth is a simple, poverty-stricken Arabic village with no industries. There is very little employment to be had in Nazareth, and living is difficult and precarious.

Miss Elsie Clor, a converted Jewess, was a worker in Jerusalem. We had some good property there, partially the gift of Northern Baptist friends and of the W. M. U. of the South. Miss Clor conducted a Good Will Center, largely for Jewish children, though the work was open also to Arabs. She had a flourishing Sabbath school on Saturday for Jewish children and a Sunday school on Sunday for all nationalities. She had clubs for boys and girls and Bible classes for women.

X

Seven Months in the Orient

On January 4, 1935, Mrs. Maddry and I sailed from San Francisco on the Dollar Line, S. S. *President Johnson,* for a visit of seven months with missions and churches in the Orient. Dr. and Mrs. J. B. Weatherspoon, of the Southern Baptist Seminary at Louisville, by invitation of the Foreign Mission Board, accompanied us. The Board was fortunate and wise in the choice of Dr. Weatherspoon as the man to accompany the Secretary on this difficult and delicate mission to the Orient. He had taught many of the younger missionaries. His help and advice were invaluable. We went out to the Orient under instructions of the Board to reorganize the work in Japan and China and bring it in line with the revised policies of the Board in Richmond.

The weather was mild and the sea was smooth during the first five days of the voyage. We spend a happy day in the semi-tropical city of Honolulu. Here we saw the strange and polyglot mixture of the races from all lands and were greatly impressed with the success of our government in its first colonial venture with Oriental people.

The first day out from Honolulu we passed the international date line. We went to bed on Tuesday night and awoke on Thursday morning. Four days off Kobe, Japan, we ran into heavy seas, and sometimes the waves were mountain high. The S. S. *President Johnson* was an old ship and creaked and groaned in every joint. There was little rest or sleep, and food had no appeal for me. Two days out of Japan, the storm reached its worst. A lady whom we had met on the boat soon after leaving San Francisco, in attempting to cross the deck, was caught by a mighty receding wave and was saved by a seaman from being swept over the stern of the boat.

Japan

Reaching Kobe on January 24, we were met by our senior missionary in Japan, Dr. W. Harvey Clarke. We had our first intimate touch with the people and life of the Japanese during the day we spent in Kobe. It was all strange and fascinating. That night we went by train to Tokyo and had our first experience of travel on the Japanese sleeping car. The trains in Japan were what we would call "narrow gauge." The berths were too narrow and short for an average sized American. Turning over in one of the berths was a difficult feat for a large-sized person.

Upon arrival in Tokyo we were greeted by missionaries Edwin Dozier and wife, Hermon Ray, and the native pastors and were entertained in the lovely home of Dr. W. Harvey Clarke. The next day we began a fifteen day tour of our Japanese Baptist churches, schools, and institutions. We found difficult problems awaiting solution. Mr. and Mrs. Dozier, Mr. Ray, and others had prepared a booklet for us giving a brief history of the Baptist work in each mission throughout Japan. The work in each church, school, and institution was described and the needs stated. A list of all missionaries who had served in Japan was given, beginning with the first Southern Baptist missionaries sent to Japan in 1889, Reverend and Mrs. J. W. McCollum and Reverend and Mrs. J. A. Brunson. A total of fifty-five had been sent out in forty-five years.

The history of modern Japan dates from 1854, when Commodore Matthew Galbraith Perry sailed into Uraga Bay, the port of modern Japan. Japan, until that time, had been a medieval, feudal kingdom, living in proud isolation from all the other nations of the world. In 1853, Secretary William A. Graham of the United States Navy, acting under the instructions of President Filmore, sent Commodore Perry to Japan on a preliminary visit. He carried a formal supplication from the president for the opening up of commercial relations between the two countries.

The Japanese government replied that the matter was of such far-reaching importance that no immediate reply could be made at that time, but that an answer would be given the following year. With the other ships of his squadron, Perry sailed away to his appointed rendezvous near Hong Kong, China. In February, 1854, he returned to Japan. His greatly enlarged squadron of "fearful fire ships" (as the Japanese called them) cast anchor over against Tokyo.

After many weeks of tiresome and evasive delay, the Japanese agreed to receive from Commodore Perry a letter and a long list of presents from President Filmore. The gifts included a miniature railway and locomotive that would run on its own steam, a telegraph set, a sewing machine, the annals of Congress, a description of bird life in America, several barrels of Kentucky whiskey, many cases of champagne, all kinds of guns and assorted ammunition for them, a list of the post offices in the United States, a Farmer's Guide, and a geological report of Minnesota!

On Sunday, July 10, 1854, negotiations concerning the treaty were suspended for the day and "divine service" was held on board the flagship of Commodore Perry. Psalm 100 was read, prayers were offered, and a group sang the great old gospel hymn which begins with the lines:

> Before Jehovah's awful throne
>   Ye nations bow with sacred joy;
> Know that the Lord is God alone,
>   He can create, He can destroy.
>
> ISAAC WATTS

The startled Japanese gathered in throngs on the shore. They were deeply impressed by this, the first Protestant Christian service ever held in Japan.

The news that Japan was at long last open to the western world created a sensation in America. Our Baptist grandfathers began to plan at once to send the gospel to the peoples of this benighted land. Missionary Matthew T. Yates of China, repeatedly urged the Foreign Mission Board to send missionaries. Dr. Yates felt so strongly that Southern Baptists should enter Japan that he offered to give up his mission in China and begin work in the Island Kingdom. So profoundly did he feel that the hour of destiny had struck for Japan that he offered to pay personally the salary of a missionary to preach the gospel in that emerging nation. The Board felt, however, that that the work of Dr. Yates in Shanghai must not be given up.

The decision was made that the Board would open work in Japan at the earliest possible time, and a diligent search was begun for a suitable couple to begin this difficult and important task.

There was subdued excitement in the mission rooms of the Baptist Foreign Mission Board in Richmond, Virginia, early in the new year of 1860. After months of seemingly fruitless search, three missionary candidates had come forward offering their services.

There was general satisfaction among the Baptists of the South and especially of Virginia, that Reverend Crawford H. Toy, a recent graduate of the University of Virginia and a student of the Southern Baptist Theological Seminary of Greenville, South Carolina, had offered to go to Japan. He was a choice young man from one of the first families of Virginia. He had taken a high rank in his studies, both at the university and at the theological seminary. He had taught for two years in the Albemarle Female Seminary in Charlottesville. It was generally understood in Baptist circles in Virginia that he was soon to marry a brilliant young woman who had recently graduated from the Albemarle Institute. It seemed the matter was all settled and was made doubly sure, when the Portsmouth Association of Virginia came forward to guarantee the salary of the young missionary.

At the same time, Reverend John Quincy Adams Rohrer, of Maryland, and his bride, Sarah Robinson Rohrer, of Pennsylvania, offered themselves for service in Japan. They were choice young people, highly educated and wholly consecrated to the missionary cause. Mrs. Rohrer was especially gifted in music.

The three promising candidates came to Richmond for examination and appointment. It was a proud and happy day among the friends of foreign missions throughout the South when the word went out that the three young people, the first to offer, had been appointed. A great throng crowded the sanctuary of the First Baptist Church of Richmond for the service where the three were solemnly set apart for the work in that far eastern land.

The Civil War suddenly burst upon the South in the spring of 1861. Mr. Toy was unable to secure passage to Japan. He became one of General Lee's chaplains and served with distinction throughout the war. Mr. and Mrs. Rohrer sailed on the *Edwin Forest* in August, 1860. On the same ship, Reverend and Mrs. A. L. Bond, newly appointed missionaries to Canton, in South China, sailed for their field of labor.

The *Edwin Forest* sailed into silence and was never heard of again. Thus ended in disappointment and tragedy the first efforts of our grandfathers to send Christ's gospel to newly-opened Japan.

It was not until the year 1889, twenty-nine years later, that work by Southern Baptist missionaries was begun in Japan—"too little and too late."

If that ship that sailed into silence had reached its destination, would the tragic aftermath for Japan have been averted? God alone knows!

When we arrived in Tokyo the weather was cold, with snow and ice on the ground. We began at once our visits to the churches. In the church and conference rooms the floors were covered with mats, and the buildings were unheated. We followed the universal Japanese custom of leaving our shoes at the door of the building and preaching in our stocking feet.

Missionary Hermon Ray had made an engagement for us to visit the noted preacher and Japanese leader, Toyohiko Kagawa. We were graciously received in his home, and he gave us two hours out of his busy life, telling us of his conversion, his labors for the cause of Christ, and the bitter persecution by former friends and governmental officials. It was indeed a rare treat to know and to have fellowship with one who after all the years of shameful persecution and imprisonment is at last universally recognized as one of the great religious leaders of his generation. It took the bitter defeat of World War II to convince the Japanese that he was the unselfish and devoted friend of all the Japanese people.

We spent a delightful day and night visiting Missionary J. Franklin Ray and wife in Hiroshima. It was a city of nearly three hundred thousand inhabitants, with beautiful parks, lakes, bridges, and attractive homes. We had an adequate church building, a faithful pastor, and a devoted congregation. In 1945 the American Air Force dropped the first atomic bomb ever made upon this city. Unknown thousands of people were killed in a flash. The horror and tragedy of modern war!

The Foreign Mission Board maintains a splendid, though limited, system of Christian education for our Baptist people in Japan.

Seinan Gakuin is our school for boys and is located in Fukuoka. It was founded by Missionary C. T. Willingham and is today one of the outstanding Christian schools for boys and young men in all Japan. In recent years the school has grown greatly in academic standards, enrolment, and physical equipment. In 1952 the total enrolment was 3483. This included the junior high, the senior high, the junior college, and the four year senior college. The woman's training school was operated in connection with the junior college and the seminary in connection with the senior college.

Seinan Jo Gakuin, the school for girls, is located at Kokura and has a splendid property on a high hill overlooking the beautiful and fast-growing city of Kokura. The W. M. U. of Japan had its offices at Kokura.

The Good Will Center at Tobata was founded by Missionary Naomi Schell of North Carolina and has been highly influential in winning all classes of Japanese people. I consider it one of the most fruitful missionary agencies that I have seen on our Baptist mission fields.

In 1935 there were only fifteen Southern Baptist missionaries for all phases of the work in Japan. Today we have more than one hundred missionaries.

Now we may look forward to a glorious day which is already dawning when the Japanese masses will turn to Christ in ever-increasing numbers. One great good, at least, that has come out of the defeat of the Japanese nation in the late war, is the declaration by the Japanese emperor himself that he is not divine and never was. Surely this opens the way to win the Japanese people to the cause of Christ and to bind this nation of seventy million alert and gifted people to our side in an all-out effort to win the billion souls in the Orient to the gospel of Christ.

America has done a thing in Japan that is unprecedented in history. She won a smashing victory over a valiant foe and then, with no thought of economic gain for herself, set them free—free from the tyranny and fear of Russia and free from their own greedy and selfish war lords. The lesson has not been lost on the Japanese people, gifted in initiative and scientific skill as few other people in the world.

China

Until this time the work in China had been organized into separate missions—the South China, the Central, the Interior, and the North China missions. Each was independent of the other, and there was no nation-wide organization. Even within the missions there was much individual action. If the missionary desired to begin a new work, he proceeded on his own responsibility and appealed directly to the Board for support. If a missionary felt led by the Lord to change from one mission to another, he went ahead and made the change without much consideration for the needs of the work as a whole. The missions were loosely tied to the Board except in the matter of support.

In each mission in China, the work was usually built up around one dominant, outstanding personality. The work had grown in a marvelous way. Schools, hospitals, and theological seminaries had sprung up and were doing good work, but there was need for a closer co-administration of the work as a whole.

While we were on a tour of our Baptist mission work in China in 1935, the deacons of the North Gate (First) Baptist Church in Shanghai placed in my hands the original minutes of the church. Here is a verbatim copy from this precious old record book of the

Charles E. Maddry and
R. T. Vann

Charles E. Maddry and
William Wallace

The Maddrys at a reception honoring his seventy-eighth birthday

Charles E. Maddry, M. Theron Rankin, and J. W. Decker, secretary, American Baptist Foreign Mission Society

first Baptist church organized in Shanghai, in the rich Yangtze Valley of Central China, where at least one hundred million people live today. The minutes are in the clear, bold handwriting of Matthew T. Yates, the first clerk of the church:

> In the Providence of God the members composing the Shanghai Baptist Mission assembled at the home of Reverend J. L. Shuck on the evening of November 6, 1847, for the purpose of constituting themselves into a church. Mr. Shuck was called to the chair and opened the meeting with prayer.
>
> The object of the meeting was then stated whereupon the following names were recorded as members of the church:
>
> Reverend J. L. Shuck
> Henrietta Hall Shuck
> Reverend Matthew Tyson Yates
> Eliza Emmeline M. Yates
> Reverend Thomas William Tobey
> Isabell Hall Tobey
> Reverend Yong Seen Sang
> Mrs. Seen Sang
>
> The above names having been presented, the church proceeded to the election of its officers, which resulted in the choice of Reverend Mr. Shuck, Moderator and pastor; Reverend Mr. Yates, Secretary; Reverend Mr. Tobey and Yong Seen Sang, Deacons.

Our first view of China left some indelible impressions upon my memory. The first was the crowds, the countless thousands crowding roadways, streets, and shops. One never gets away from the crowds. One wonders where they live, how they live, and what hope there is of ever winning these throngs to Christ's way of life. After seeing the multitudes of China, one can have a better understanding of the experiences of Jesus: Seeing the multitudes he was moved with compassion toward them, because they were like sheep having no shepherd. He always did something about it. But, however much one's heart may be moved by the sight of the crowds of the Orient, the baffling question remains to haunt one's hours, "What can be done about it?" The crowds! Multitudes that no man can number!

The second impression still lingers with me: the sight of the throngs of ragged, hungry, hopeless beggars. They were everywhere with their piteous pleas for money with which to buy a little rice. At first, overwhelmed with their cry, I began to give out the small supply of coins I had, but it was soon exhausted. Then a missionary rescued me from the pressing throngs and reminded me that I could not feed even a small part of the hungry crowd that pressed upon us with their appeals. Always, everywhere we heard the multitude of beggars pleading for food!

Another picture that I cannot forget was that of the toiling, sweating thousands carrying heavy burdens and doing the work of beasts. One often saw a wagon or truck heavily loaded with stone, structural steel, or other building material, being drawn at a snail's pace upgrade by a struggling, sweating group of little men and women. Some would be pulling at the tongue of a heavy wagon with grass ropes over their shoulders, while others would be pushing and straining at the wheels. Often there would be a mother with a baby strapped on her back pulling or pushing the heavy load. What was the reward? After the long day of such toil was over, there might be enough money to buy a little food for the family.

Another impression was the sight of a poorly-clad, underpaid, and undernourished Chinese man, pulling a wealthy Chinese gentleman or an American business man in his ricksha, trotting three miles for ten cents in American money. The men who follow this business are short-lived. They die early of heart disease or pneumonia, contracted while waiting so thinly clad in the cold for another "fare." I shall never forget my first ride in a ricksha. I started to the hospital to see one of our missionaries who was sick. The ricksha man I selected gave out before I was half-way. He fell in the street with a heart attack. I can see today the look of misery and helpless appeal in his eyes as I pressed into his trembling hand more than the amount of his fare for the full distance of the trip. Frankly, I never could feel comfortable riding behind a fellow human being, pulling us at a trot like a horse.

In Shanghai were centered nearly all the executive and financial agencies of our four China missions, Central, South, Interior, and North. Here, in a five-story office building owned by the Foreign Mission Board, were the headquarters offices for all our mission work in China. Here, also, was located our China Baptist Publication Society and printing outfit, which supplied all the literature for the churches, Sunday schools, missionary societies, colleges, and theological seminaries of all China. A large book store was in this building, too.

One of the greatest evangelistic agencies Baptists had in China was here in Shanghai. The University of Shanghai, owned, staffed, and controlled jointly by American and Southern Baptists, was the first educational institution of higher learning in all China to open its doors to men and women alike, a step that was revolutionary in the history of higher education in China. The University, together with its affiliated School of Theology and its downtown School of Commerce and Business Administration, gave to Baptists a commanding position in educational circles in China not surpassed by any other in all China. These combined institutions trained the pastors, the school and college teachers, and a vast number of outstanding leaders in business and industry throughout the country.

In Shanghai were located also several noted and popular primary and preparatory schools for boys and girls. Outstanding among these was the school for girls, founded seventy-five years ago by Mrs. Matthew T. Yates, and conducted under the auspices of the famous old North Gate Church. After Mrs. Yates' death, the school was carried on by Miss Willie Kelly, assisted in later years by Miss Pearle Johnson of North Carolina.

The Eliza Yates School for Girls and the Ming Jang School for Boys served the young people of Shanghai and attracted students from afar. Here Dr. R. T. Bryan gave the last years of his long and fruitful missionary career in China.

In 1935 there were many fast-growing and influential churches in Shanghai and in the vast Yangtze River area round about. It seemed to us that the ninety years of seed-sowing in that strategic center were beginning to bear bountiful fruit and that the churches were ready to reap a rich harvest of souls for the kingdom of God. The missionaries conducted us to the top of a famous and unique peak that thrusts its head more than a hundred feet above the vast alluvial plain near Quinsan, some fifty miles up the Yangtze River from Shanghai. Here on this peak Dr. Yates often retired for prayer and meditation.

A few weeks after I reached China, I became aware of a growing sense of nationalism and of a wide-spread longing among the Chinese leaders and churches for an all-China Baptist unity to be expressed in the organization of a national Chinese Baptist convention. After consultations with Baptist leaders from both the Northern and Southern Conventions, together with leaders in all phases of native Baptist life, we came to the conclusion that the time had come to put into effect the organization of an all-China Baptist convention, embracing every phase of Baptist work.

Dr. Weatherspoon and I left Shanghai for a visit of some ten days among the churches in Shantung Province—a visit which was highly valuable in helping us understand and appreciate the wonderful growth and development of our Baptist churches and institutions throughout this great Chinese province. We received a royal welcome wherever we went and were highly pleased to see the rapid growth of our work in North China.

One experience we had in Tsinan, the capital of Shantung Province, was very inspiring. Missionary Frank Connely had sent out a call to the churches for a meeting of their representatives with the visitors from the headquarters of the Richmond office. Pastors and leaders in the churches came in large numbers. Some came as far as forty miles to this conference; they brought their food and bedding on their backs and slept in heathen temples by the way. There were several leaders of women's work among the delegations, some of whom had walked weary miles over frozen roads on their small, bound, doll-like feet that they might add their plea to that of the men for reinforcements. From nine until one o'clock we heard these delegations, and the one plea of all was the same: "Send us missionaries and Chinese evangelists to preach the gospel, for the fields are white unto the harvest." We heard over and over in this plea of every delegation, "Send us missionaries with hot hearts."

After this hasty trip, we were more fully convinced than ever that the time had come to give to the growing sense of nationalism on the part of the China Baptists the influence and encouragement of the Foreign Mission Board of the Southern Baptist Convention. We returned to Shanghai and after further conferences with missionaries and native leaders sent out a call to all our Baptist missionaries and native leaders of China for a conference in Shanghai early in April. While the Foreign Mission Board paid the traveling expenses of our missionaries, the churches, national boards and schools paid the expenses of the Chinese representatives.

They came in large numbers—missionaries, pastors, and leaders—representing all Baptist work in China, both American and Southern. Heretofore, the missionaries had scarcely known their fellow missionaries except those belonging to their own mission. The native pastors and leaders were likewise meeting for the first time. It was truly a conference of far-reaching import for our mission work in China. Instead of a limited and circumscribed view of the work as the responsibility of only one provincial mission, a vision of the work as the united responsibility of all the Baptist forces in China was to grow out of this conference.

Out of this meeting in Shanghai, the Secretary and the missionaries received a new impression of the worth and ability of our Chinese coworkers in an all-out effort to win China to Christ. Before this, we had a feeling that the task of winning the Chinese to Christ was largely the duty and responsibility of the Board in Richmond and of the missionaries in China. With a new appreciation of our Chinese churches and leaders, there came to all of us a new sense of the vital need for co-operation. Henceforth, the main burden of the task was to rest upon the Chinese churches and leaders, and we were to be partners and helpers in the undertaking. It was no longer a *foreign* mission enterprise carried on by Americans, but a Chinese enterprise in which we were to co-operate with them and reinforce them in their *home* mission enterprise.

The Communists have shut us out of China for a season, but God is still at work behind the Bamboo Curtain, and multitudes of Chinese Baptists remain faithful.

We visited the churches and missionary friends in the ancient city of Soochow where strong churches and efficient schools were located. Yates Academy for boys and Weiling Academy for girls were not only schools of high academic standing, but they were, above all, evangelistic. Dr. and Mrs. C. G. McDaniel, Miss Sophie Lanneau, and many other consecrated missionaries wrought nobly in teaching young Chinese the way of life.

We spent four weeks of difficult travel and of fine fellowship with the churches and workers in these two great missions in Interior and North China. It was a rare and inspiring experience that was to guide us during the dark and difficult days that were to come to all of our mission work in China, for, henceforth, we were to be the *Big Brother*, co-operating and reinforcing them where they were weak.

When we were in Chefoo, North China, Missionary J. Walton Moore took us out one day to a near-by Chinese village to visit the monument erected by that heathen village to the memory of the beloved Southern Baptist missionary, J. L. Holmes. When we came to the edge of the village, we saw in a near-by wheat field an imposing marble slab. On one side in Chinese characters was an elaborate inscription, with an English translation of the same on the other side. It told, in eloquent detail, the story of the heroic and supreme sacrifice of the white missionary—one who had come from beyond the western seas, bringing a new and strange religion. It told how he had made every effort to save the adjacent village from the cruel wrath of the Taiping rebels.

Preceding the All-China Conference in Shanghai we spent six weeks in Canton and the South China area. The first missionaries sent to China by American Baptists were located in Canton—J. L. Shuck and Henrietta Hall Shuck, T. J. Roberts, and Samuel C. Clopton and wife. Henrietta Hall Shuck, the first woman missionary to enter China, was a gifted woman but lived only a few years after reaching China. She is buried in Hong Kong.

Samuel C. Clopton, the first missionary appointed by the newly-created Foreign Mission Board of the Southern Baptist Convention, September 1, 1845, lived only a short time. He died July 7, 1847, and is buried near Canton.

In Canton was located the Graves Theological Seminary, named for the gallant missionary, Dr. R. H. Graves, who gave some forty years of brilliant and devoted service to our cause in Canton. Dr. M. T. Rankin was the efficient and worthy president of this growing seminary at the time of our visit.

The Baptist hospital was under the management of Dr. C. A. Hayes, an official of the South China Baptist Convention. The National Convention also sponsored an orphanage which was entirely supported by the Chinese churches. Mrs. Hayes, also a skilled and accomplished physician, operated a highly successful clinic for girls and women in the city. Since increasing numbers of girls and women came to this clinic to be treated, it had developed into a great evangelistic agency.

The hospital had won its way into the hearts of the people not only of Canton, but also of all the regions round about. Dr. Hayes, a brilliant physician, had wide renown as a surgeon in all kinds of diseases of the eyes. Government officials and war lords from all over a vast area came to him for treatment. Withal, he was a friend of the poor and needy and never turned one away from his hospital if he was sick or destitute. Both he and his wife were great soul-winners, and no patient who came to the hospital was dismissed without an earnest effort being made to win him to Christ.

There were many churches and missions and schools in Canton and the suburban areas. The First Church, which had some two thousand members led by a gifted and highly educated Chinese pastor, ministered to great crowds. It had a large choir—one of the best we found in all China.

Mrs. Janie Sanford Graves, of Blue Mountain, Mississippi, the widow of R. H. Graves, conducted a well-known school for blind girls. Blindness is widely prevalent all over South China. The great heart of Mrs. Graves was deeply moved for this unfortunate group. Girls are often unwanted and the hopeless plight of these miserable children was pitiable indeed. Mrs. Graves, supported by gifts from the women of Mississippi, supplemented by the Foreign Mission Board, had gathered about her a splendid, capable staff of missionaries and Chinese teachers. The school began in a modest way, but when I visited Canton, it had grown into an efficient missionary agency which attracted blind girls from all classes, rich and poor alike, from a wide area. Nothing I saw in China moved me more than this wonderful Christian service being rendered by Mrs. Graves and her associates.

Another appealing work was being done by Miss Lydia Greene in the teaching of a large number of Chinese children in her kindergarten school. It began, like all our mission work, in a modest way but had grown to imposing proportions and was then a training school for teachers. It was a beautiful and impressive sight to see this devoted American missionary and her Chinese helpers whom she had trained giving themselves unselfishly to this work.

A little later when the Japanese armies overran and devastated South China, there was great misery and suffering among all classes of the Chinese. Since the suffering was especially bitter and severe among the helpless little children of Canton, this devoted missionary stayed on and with gifts from friends in America and the Foreign Mission Board was able to save hundreds of these little ones from starvation and death. She set up a feeding station and was able to buy with American money, food sufficient to give her little charges one good, nourishing meal a day. Communism soon overran Canton, as well as all China, but it was never able to beat out the glorious work done by Lydia Greene for the suffering children of her city.

Large and flourishing schools were conducted by the South China Mission for both boys and girls. The faculties were composed of missionaries and Chinese teachers. Large numbers of young people were prepared in these schools for entrance into advanced schools, both American and Chinese. In fact, many of these students went on to our own Baptist University in Shanghai for further training.

I have already spoken of the work being done in our hospital in Canton by Dr. and Mrs. Hayes. I spent several days in Wuchow visiting the churches and the hospital there. Dr. George W. Leavell had done a splendid work through this hospital. When his health failed, the Board sent Dr. and Mrs. R. E. Beddoe, of Texas, to take up the work. They did a magnificent and far-reaching work in this strategic and fast-growing city. When they were transferred, the

Board sent Dr. William Wallace who was highly successful in enlarging and extending the work, not only in the city, but throughout a wide area in Southwestern China. He became widely known and was greatly beloved by the Chinese of all classes.

When the Communists overran Wuchow in 1950, Dr. Wallace was arrested and accused of being an American spy. He was isolated and treated with inhuman cruelty. In an effort to secure evidence to back up their charges that he was a spy, the Communists paraded Dr. Wallace through the streets of the city and the outlying areas, clothed only in his pajamas. Every effort was made to induce the Chinese, especially the Christians, to come forward and testify against him. After weeks of torture to get him to confess to the trumped-up charges that he was a spy, he was murdered in his cell. After this, his lifeless body was hanged by the neck, and it was given out that he had died by suicide. The mutilated body was then turned over to the Christians, who sorrowfully buried him in the Christian cemetery in Wuchow. It was one of the most brutal murders ever committed in the history of missions.

There was universal sorrow and regret over the resignation of Dr. M. T. Rankin as president of the Graves Theological Seminary to serve as regional secretary for the Orient, with offices in Shanghai. The Mission was somewhat comforted when we announced that a new missionary would be sent out for the presidency of the Graves Theological Seminary. Missionary Eugene Hill and his wife took up the work of the seminary.

Dr. Rankin did a splendid work in his new task of supervising all our work in Japan and China, serving in this capacity with success and general acceptance until the Japanese overran China. Along with many more of our China missionaries, he was thrown into a miserable concentration camp in Hong Kong. I did not see it all then, but God, the Author of missions, had in training in the bitter school of adversity, the future Executive Secretary of the Foreign Mission Board.

In 1903, when the Foreign Mission Board decided that the time had come to extend its work into the interior of China, Missionary W. W. Lawton, a native of South Carolina, was chosen to lead in this new endeavor. In the fall of that year, W. Eugene Sallee, a native of Kentucky and a graduate of our Louisville seminary was appointed to join Mr. Lawton in this new and challenging undertaking in the interior of China. He was a young man of outstanding ability, wholly committed to mission work in China. Honan Province, with a population of thirty-five million people, was selected as the field for the new mission work. Missionaries Lawton and Sallee traveled hundreds of miles by river boats and other slow means to reach the destination of their new work. The last fifteen miles were covered on foot; their baggage was carried in wheel barrows pushed by coolies. Mr. Lawton already knew the language, and Mr. Sallee with the aid of a native teacher began at once the difficult work of learning to preach in a strange tongue.

Kaifeng, the important capital of the province, and the near-by city of Chengchow were the outposts for the work of the missionaries, a work which in the years to come was to grow into one of the greatest mission undertakings in all China.

In a week's time after reaching Chengchow the missionaries found a location and began work. They rented a good-sized compound, arranged living quarters in the rear, and fixed up the front, which faced a prominent street, for a preaching place. Mr. Lawton began preaching at once, with Mr. Sallee assisting in every way possible. In addition to his language study, he distributed tracts and invited the people to the services.

The work grew from the beginning, and soon the little chapel was filled with attentive listeners. Finally, Mrs. Lawton and the two little girls, after many hardships of travel, reached Chengchow. A small, crude home had been fitted up by Mr. Lawton, and the work took on new impetus when he was freed for more devoted effort in the work of preaching. The Chinese crowded the chapel and soon overflowed into the home. They were curious and greatly interested in their first sight of a foreign woman and the little American girls. Soon a new missionary, Mr. A. Y. Napier, was sent out to join this tiny group in the far interior of China. After Mr. Sallee had completed the first phase of language study, he was able to begin preaching in Chinese.

On September 18, 1906, Mr. Sallee and Miss Annie Jenkins, of Waco, Texas, were married in Shanghai in the home of Miss Willie Kelly. Mr. Frank Rawlinson, a classmate of Mr. Sallee, performed the ceremony. After a stay of one week in Shanghai, Mr. and Mrs. Sallee went to Chengchow.

On September 5, 1907, Mr. Sallee baptized four converts, his first time to perform this sacred ordinance in China. About this time, Mr. and Mrs. D. W. Herring, who had been working with the Gospel Mission, came to our Board and were sent to Chengchow. The Board decided to expand, and to enter the large and important city of Kaifeng, the capital of Honan Province, six miles from the Yellow River. Mr. and Mrs. Sallee were selected for the work, the move being made in 1908. The Sunday after their arrival in the city, the first service was held with a congregation of five people. When the men asked Mr. Sallee about the crops, the products, the habits, and the customs of the people in America, his reply was, "Well, they are civilized in the United States just as we are."

Honan Province, with its teeming millions, was almost entirely dependent upon agriculture. Wheat was the main crop, and the yield was often poor. Famine, with its trials, suffering, and disease, was a constant threat to the lives of the people. Mr. Sallee, who had been reared in the rich bluegrass of Kentucky, where there were abundant harvests with prosperity and plenty on every hand, soon conceived the idea of improving the yield of wheat by improving the quality of the seed. He began the slow process of selecting year by year the best wheat available. The agricultural authorities of the provincial college gladly co-operated with him in this undertaking, the object before the Kaifeng College being to improve the yield of all food crops, especially wheat.

The missionaries of the Interior Mission soon found that one of the big problems facing them was the securing of an adequate milk supply, for they were dependent upon the very uncertain and meager supply obtained from a flock of goats. They first experimented with native cows but found this unsatisfactory. Cows, used for plowing the fields, gave little milk and were rarely used for meat unless they were diseased or too old to pull a plow. A quart of milk a day was the average supply furnished by one cow.

Mr. Sallee conceived the idea of bringing in a small herd of the very best milk cows to be had in America. On his furlough in 1919, he visited a number of the big breeders of dairy cattle in America. He told them of his dreams and plans for securing a small herd of registered milk cows to take back with him to his mission in China.

The missionary had a sympathetic response from the cattle breeders of America to his appeal for help in carrying out his dream of building up the food supply of his adopted people in China. He secured from donations, mainly from the North, twenty-two head of fine blooded cattle—eleven Holsteins and eleven Jerseys. Money enough was also given for the transportation of his cattle to interior China. En route to China the cattle became infected with rinderpest germs, and in two weeks after arriving in Kaifeng the cows began to die. Soon all but five were dead. However, Mr. Sallee was not discouraged, and in a few months his fine purebreds had increased to fifteen pure and seventeen half-breeds, worth at least six thousand dollars in American money. Best of all, the people began to learn to drink milk. Soon many Chinese families, besides foreigners, were being furnished with rich milk.

The cattle industry grew and the provincial government was greatly impressed with the success of this new mission project. Nothing ever undertaken by these resourceful missionaries made a finer impression upon the pagan people of China for the gospel of Christ, than these practical steps to help feed the starving people.

As we write these words our missionaries are restricted in their labors to Hong Kong and adjacent areas in Baptist territory. Since 1949 Chinese refugees have been pouring into Hong Kong from mainland China's eighteen provinces. There are now eight Baptist churches in this city of nearly 2,500,000 population. The oldest church with continued existence is Cheung Chow, organized in 1842.

Our missionaries formerly working in China have been deployed to other areas in the Orient where millions of Chinese and other people may be reached, Formosa, Philippines, Korea, Thailand, Malaya, and Indonesia. This reminds us of New Testament days, when they that were scattered abroad by persecution "went everywhere preaching the word."

XI

Down Under the Southern Cross

SOUTHERN BAPTISTS began work in Brazil in 1881, when Reverend and Mrs. W. B. Bagby, of Texas, appointed by our Foreign Mission Board in December, 1880, were the first Baptist missionaries to enter the country.

After the defeat of the South in the Civil War, there were many in the deep South who felt they could never again live in happiness under the stars and stripes. Colonies from South Carolina, Georgia, Louisiana, Mississippi, and Texas went out to Brazil to raise coffee and cotton with slave labor. The main center of operations for these self-exiled Southerners was at Santa Barbara, near São Paulo, Southern Brazil. Here they organized a Baptist church where their own group might worship. Upon the arrival of Mr. and Mrs. Bagby in Rio Janeiro, they found a letter from this little Baptist group in Santa Barbara, inviting them to come and preach for the church while they were studying the language. Accepting the invitation, they found a royal welcome awaiting them from these homesick exiles from Dixie.

In 1882, Reverend and Mrs. Z. C. Taylor were sent out by the Foreign Mission Board to join the Bagbys at Santa Barbara. They spent a year here in preaching and in studying Portuguese. As soon as they felt that they had acquired a working knowledge of the language, they decided to go more than a thousand miles to Bahia, the most antagonistic Catholic city in Brazil. The Catholics in Bahia claim that they have 365 churches in the city of 400,000 people, one for every day of the year. I do not vouch for the truth of this claim, but I do know that wherever one turns in Bahia, there is a Catholic church steeple.

Late in October, 1882, the missionaries at Bahia organized the first Brazilian Baptist church. Having made a beginning in a great city in the north, they decided that the time had come to launch a

Baptist mission in Rio de Janeiro, the capital of the country. The Bagbys, leaving the Taylors in charge of the newly-organized work in Bahia, went to Rio and began our work there in 1883. In 1884, after many trying experiences and in the face of bitter persecution on the part of the Catholics, the Bagbys organized a Baptist church. Now there are nearly one hundred Baptist churches in Rio.

In May, 1936, the Foreign Mission Board authorized the Executive Secretary to visit our missions in South America and to select a Baptist leader to accompany him on an inspection tour of our work in the lands of South America. I selected Dr. L. R. Scarborough, president of the Southwestern Theological Seminary at Fort Worth, to go with me. He and Mrs. Scarborough made the trip at their own expense.

Our party, in addition to Dr. and Mrs. Scarborough, consisted of Dr. W. C. Taylor, secretary for our work in Latin America, Mrs. Taylor and their twelve-year-old daughter Betty, Mrs. Maddry, and Miss Mary Shepherd, secretary to Dr. Taylor.

Brazil

We caught our first sight of South America on June 1 and two days later sailed into Rio de Janeiro, the most beautiful harbor we have seen in the world.

Here began some six weeks of mission conferences, preaching engagements, and fellowship with a glorious company of devoted and courageous missionaries. With Rio as a center, we visited our churches and schools in the outlying areas, making fruitful contacts with all phases of our work in the city, the Federal District, and the state of Rio.

The annual Mission meeting for all South Brazil was held in Rio. At these meetings, reports are presented from all stations and mission points. The meetings, much like associational meetings in the homeland, usually last about a week. They are of great social and spiritual value, especially for the missionaries who are serving in isolated stations in the interior. At this time the needs of every field are carefully canvassed, and requests for appropriations are sent up to the Board in Richmond as well as requests for new missionary recruits and replacements. This meeting was of special importance.

The outstanding business of the Mission meeting was the dedication of the new building for the Carroll Memorial Publishing House, which had been under construction for some months. This publishing house has been one of the greatest evangelizing agencies in all South America. All the Portuguese literature, books, and tracts for our Baptist work in Brazil are published there.

A meeting of the National Baptist Convention for all Brazil was held in the city of Recife during the latter part of June. Nearly all the missionaries attended the annual meeting, and a large number of native pastors, laymen, and women came from all parts of Brazil.

Our party was welcomed with great enthusiasm. It was a meeting of far-reaching importance, and plans were made for advancement in all departments of work of the Convention. The Executive Secretary was heard with deep interest as he outlined plans for closer cooperation between the Brazilian Convention and the sponsoring Board in North America. We found the Convention ready to assume a larger part than ever before in the plans for the support of the work. The seed-sowing of fifty years on the part of the North American Foreign Mission Board was beginning to pay rich dividends in the promise of the national churches to assume a larger share in the evangelization of their own people.

It was ten o'clock in the evening and the National Convention was just getting under way. The president had told Dr. Scarborough that he would call on him to pronounce the benediction when the Convention adjourned. In the president's speech, made in Portuguese, he mentioned the names of the visitors and upon hearing his name called Dr. Scarborough arose and dismissed the Convention. There was a good laugh all around, and the visitor enjoyed the joke as much as the Brazilians.

At the close of the meeting of the National Convention, we went home with Mr. and Mrs. M. G. White of Bahia. We were especially impressed with the work that was carried on by Mrs. White among the leading young women of Catholic faith. The missionary had organized a class in cooking and sewing, and the young daughters of wealthy families came in large numbers to learn the art of homemaking from the cultured and gifted missionary of the despised little Baptist group. Though the Catholic priest had done his best to prevent the young matrons of his parish from attending the school of this young missionary, through the influence of the classes many doors were being opened into the homes of leading Catholic families of the city.

We had an engagement in Victoria, a city about half-way between Bahia and Pernambuco (Recife) but found that there was no boat schedule that would enable us to reach our engagement at the appointed time. Having never traveled by airplane, Dr. Scarborough and I were very reluctant to make the trip by air. Rather than miss our engagement in Victoria, we left our wives to join us later by boat in Rio, and took to the air for the dreaded trip to Victoria. I was like the colored brother who went up for his first flight. When he landed safely, a friend asked him if he was scared. He replied that he was not scared because "he never did quite rest all his weight on the strange thing." However, we made the trip safely and met our engagement on time. After a delightful visit with the missionaries in Victoria where Mrs. Reno was still serving, we returned by hydroplane to Rio. While we were in North Brazil our schedule did not permit us to go up into the Amazon Valley, now the Equatorial Mission where the veteran E. A. Nelson wrought so faithfully many years.

In a few days we left Rio for a visit with our missionaries and churches in the great interior state of Minas. This state, which is as large as Texas, is fabulously rich in minerals and grazing lands. A great center for cattle raising, it is destined to be one of the wealthiest states in all Brazil.

When we reached Belo Horizonte, the missionaries and a large group of native pastors, leading women, and students of the Baptist college gave us a royal welcome. We were entertained in the lovely home of Mr. and Mrs. Maddox. We had been students together in the Louisville seminary in 1904 and 1905. The Maddox family is remarkable, not only in missionary service and achievement, but in giving to the cause of Christ four preachers, all four of whom became chaplains in World War II.

The Baptist college in Belo Horizonte has grown in a marvelous way. The only Baptist college in this vast state of Minas, it has a magnificent campus on a high hill overlooking the beautiful capital of the state. There are several churches in the city, and our work under the direction of Evangelist J. R. Allen is rapidly spreading into the interior of this great state.

From Belo Horizonte, we journeyed to São Paulo, the second city in Brazil and one of the great cities of South America. The state of São Paulo, marvelously rich in coffee, cotton, and timber, is rapidly growing into a great industrial empire. The population is overwhelmingly white—Spanish, Italian, and North European. Moreover, it is one of the most beautiful cities in the Western Hemisphere.

The Baptist work has grown and expanded in a wonderful way

throughout the whole state. Paul Porter was for years the only field missionary in São Paulo. We have some splendid and influential churches in the city. There is a good church at Santos, the seaport of São Paulo and the largest coffee exporting port in the world. From this great port, ships go to all the world, carrying precious cargoes of coffee, cattle, leather, and mahogany, as well as a vast number of manufactured products.

In São Paulo we have a large and fast-growing high school for girls. The school with its splendid group of buildings is centrally located and draws girls from the well-to-do families of the city and state of São Paulo. Reverend and Mrs. F. A. R. Morgan, the principals of the school, were assisted by Misses Mattie Baker, Essie Fuller, and Alma Jackson. The workers in the state at large were Reverend and Mrs. T. C. Bagby. Since our visit, several other missionaries have been sent to the state of São Paulo.

Our stay in São Paulo was all too short, but engagements were waiting for us at Curityba and Porto Alegre. In Curityba we had blessed fellowship with missionaries Mr. and Mrs. A. B. Deter and Mr. and Mrs. A. B. Oliver. Mrs. Oliver is the daughter of Dr. and Mrs. Deter. Dr. Deter had general oversight of the evangelistic work, while Mr. Oliver had charge of the training school for preachers. The work here was making splendid progress in the fast growing city.

Dr. Deter, a splendid missionary and a remarkable man in other ways, had faced bitter persecution from the Catholic priests; and the people greatly admired him for his courage and devotion to the right. He had acquired Brazilian citizenship, and was made a chaplain with the rank of captain in the Brazilian Army. The fact that he had served with distinction greatly added to his effectiveness as a missionary.

Our next stop was at the most southern mission station of our Board in Brazil. Here were located Dr. and Mrs. W. B. Bagby, the founders of our work in Brazil. They were living in useful retirement with their daughter, Miss Helen Bagby, who married Missionary W. E. Harrison in 1939. We spent ten days in their lovely home. Four of their children and a granddaughter have become missionaries in Latin America. Alice married Harley Smith, and, at the time we were there, they were engaged in school and evangelistic work. Albert, the youngest son, married a missionary and located in Porto Alegre. Reverend T. C. Bagby and wife are evangelistic missionaries in the state of São Paulo. Thus the Bagby family, together with the sons,

sons-in-law, daughters-in-law, and a granddaughter in Argentina, (Mrs. Anna Sowell Margrett), have given to Baptists a total of thirteen missionaries. I doubt if there is another Baptist family in the South that has made such a contribution to the missionary cause as the Bagby family.

Brazilian Baptists have both a Home Mission Board, organized in 1907, and a Foreign Mission Board. Dr. L. M. Bratcher, for many years Secretary of the Home Mission Board, was called to a glorious reward in December, 1953.

We left South Brazil on a German hydroplane known as a Condor and landed in the harbor of the beautiful city of Montevideo, capital of Uruguay, on a cold day in mid-winter—about the middle of August.

Uruguay

The Republic of Uruguay is a small country, if we consider only population and size. Despite constant pressure from its big neighbor just across the river, Rio de la Plata, Uruguay has managed to remain one of the most democratic and progressive states in all South America.

Uruguay is a vast rolling plain, rising slightly in the north. The rivers, Rio de la Plata, Rio Negro, and Uruguay furnish easy communication by water for the entire country, while the nation has a 130-mile Atlantic shoreline.

Uruguay is often called the Switzerland of South America because of the stability of its government and the soundness of its currency. It has never been cursed with the oft-recurring political revolutions that harass and paralyze other South American countries.

Our Baptist work in Uruguay, which was small, was organized as a part of the Argentine Mission. In Montevideo, we had two missionaries—Mr. and Mrs. B. W. Orrick. Our main work was in the capital city where we had two good churches and several missions rapidly growing into churches.

Argentina

The next stop on our mission tour was Argentina. The principal cities are Buenos Aires, with a population of 3,000,371, and Rosario, with 461,688 inhabitants. The republic is comprised of fourteen provinces with ten territories. It is second in size to Brazil. In general, the country is a plain, rising westward from the Atlantic to the Chilean border and the towering peaks, including Aconcagua which is 23,081 feet high, the highest peak in the world outside Asia. The climate is mild in winter and torrid in summer. The three great rivers forming the Plata system, the Parana, Paraguay, and the Uruguay, are important commercial arteries in northern Argentina.

Don Pablo Besson was born in Switzerland in 1848. His father was a distinguished pastor in the state church (the Presbyterian in that canton). His mother was a descendant of the Waldensians of northern Italy. He was highly educated and, from his youth, was a fighting advocate of absolute religious liberty. While studying for the Presbyterian ministry, he experienced a revolutionary change that finally led into the fellowship of a small group of despised Baptists. He was baptized by Reverend J. B. Critin, a French pastor. For a time he served as a missionary of the American Baptist Mission Board in France and Belgium. Then learning of a great spiritual destitution in Catholic-dominated South America, he came to Argentina. His father never forgave him for joining the despised and persecuted sect known as Baptists.

Mr. Besson had not been in Argentina long before he realized that Baptists would always be at a serious disadvantage in the Argentine Republic unless some fundamental changes should be made in the laws of the country. Some of the young people of his flock wanted to marry, but the marrying business was a monopoly of the Roman Catholic priests. If a Baptist couple wanted to marry legally, they must first go to confession, that is, become Catholics. Also, the priest always made the fee prohibitive for the poor Baptists. Then, when one died, he could not be buried in the "holy ground" of a Catholic cemetery.

Mr. Besson realized that the very existence of the Baptists in Argentina was in peril until the laws of the land were changed, and his people, along with all Protestants, were granted religious freedom and decent human rights before the law. In 1888, the National Congress passed a bill establishing the civil register of births, marriages, and deaths for all citizens alike. No longer were the masses under the tyranny of the Catholic priesthood. Thus, Don Pablo Besson was the author of religious liberty for all the people of Argentina for all time. This noble patriot passed to his eternal reward in 1932. He was truly the founder of our Baptist work in Argentina.

There were other worthy Baptists who came from Europe in the early days to reinforce the labor of Mr. Besson. They were not connected with any mission board but usually taught school and preached on the side. The first of these was Reverend George Graham, an English Baptist, who located in the town of Las Flores in the Province of Buenos Aires. Here he conducted a boarding school for a living and preached as opportunity afforded. Another English Baptist, Frederick L. Newton, came out on faith, giving part time to teaching school and preaching as the occasion arose. Few families have made a greater contribution to the spiritual life of the Argentine, than the French family of Don Alberto Osterman. He was a merchant, and was converted under the preaching of Don Besson. Soon his two sons, Gabriel and Julio, were converted and began to preach also. Another early stalwart in preaching was Don Jogrin Otero, a Spaniard. He joined forces with Don Pablo Besson and was the organizing genius of our Baptist cause in those early days.

There was a growing conviction on the part of many Southern Baptists that they should begin work in Argentina. For twenty years Mr. Besson had been praying and pleading for help from the Foreign Mission Board of the Southern Baptist Convention. Just at this time Reverend Sidney M. Sowell, a choice young man from Virginia, offered himself for this work. There was one difficulty in the way of appointing Mr. Sowell—he did not have a wife! It had been the policy of the Foreign Mission Board not to appoint an unmarried man as a missionary. Dr. Willingham, the Secretary, solved the problem by securing from Mr. Sowell the promise that on his way to Argentina, he would stop off at São Paulo, where Dr. W. B. Bagby and his family were laboring. The oldest daughter of Dr. Bagby was teaching in the São Paulo Girls' School. Mr. Sowell, true to his promise, stopped over for a two weeks visit with the Bagbys. It was love at first sight! Soon Miss Bagby became Mrs. Sowell, and in Buenos Aires they spent forty years together in happy and fruitful missionary service. Their daughter is now a missionary of our Board and is superintendent of the Argentina W. M. U. Training School.

About the same time, the Board appointed Reverend and Mrs. J. L. Hart, Reverend and Mrs. K. W. Cawthon, Reverend and Mrs. Frank J. Fowler as fellow laborers with the Sowells in Argentina. At long last, there was a strong and aggressive Baptist missionary work firmly established in the three republics facing the Atlantic—all the way from northern Brazil to Tierra del Fuego.

We reached Argentina about July 15. It was mid-winter and cold. The churches were all without heat, and the floors were of tile. We preached in cold auditoriums, wearing heavy flannels, overcoats, and rubbers. The missionary homes were inadequately heated, and we really suffered with cold.

The annual meeting of the River Plate Mission was held in Buenos Aires and was an interesting and inspiring occasion. The missionaries of Paraguay and Uruguay were members of the Argentine Mission.[1] Plans for enlargement and new missionary recruits were made, and all together it was an enthusiastic and forward-looking meeting.

Chile

We crossed the Andes by Pan-Air, and it was a thrilling and inspiring experience as the plane went up to eighteen thousand feet to get through the snow-covered gorges. We landed in the beautiful capital of Chile, Santiago, which is a city of 1,161,633 inhabitants.

The Baptists have laid a splendid foundation in Chile, and with the large number of ardent new missionaries being sent out by our Board, before long the whole spiritual condition will be transformed. The domination of the Catholic Church over the masses of the population is slowly but surely being broken.

Early missionaries in Chile in addition to Reverend W. D. T. MacDonald, the Scotchman, were Dr. and Mrs. R. C. Moore, Reverend and Mrs. J. L. Hart, transferred from the Argentine Mission, Reverend and Mrs. J. W. McGavock, Reverend and Mrs. W. E. Maier, and Misses Agnes Graham, Cornelia Brower, Anne Laseter, and Marjorie Spence.

We met with the missionaries in their annual meeting and laid plans for the enlargement of the work in buildings and new missionary recruits. It was decided to open a new mission in Antofagasta, in the mining district to the north. We visited the churches in Santiago, Temuco, Concepcion, Valparaiso, and other cities.

We have an efficient theological seminary and a splendid school for girls, the Colegio Bautista, founded at Temuco by Agnes Graham, which is fast transforming the young womanhood of all Chile.

Among the cherished memories of our visit was the glorious work done by Agnes Graham during her twenty-seven years in Chile from the time she was appointed in June, 1920, until she was called to her heavenly home January 23, 1946. I have recalled many times that Sunday morning in October, 1916, how, after I had preached in the University Baptist Church, Austin, on "The Upward Calling," beautiful Agnes Graham heard God's call and came forward.

---

[1] In 1952 Paraguay was organized as a separate mission.

She was a junior in the university and a brilliant and outstanding student. As the pastor took her hand, her lovely face was suffused with tears, and she said gently but firmly: "I will go to the ends of the earth as He shall lead."

Agnes Graham finished her course in the university with high honors and went on to the Woman's Missionary Union Training School at Louisville, Kentucky, where she graduated with distinction in 1920.

With her background of culture and scholarship, it was easy for her to master the Spanish language, and in a few years she was speaking with the ease and fluency of a native. She was a born teacher and had the innate ability of inspiring enthusiasm and loyal devotion in all who came under her tuition.

Some years prior to her arrival in Chile, Reverend W. D. T. MacDonald, a rugged and courageous Scotchman, had begun an independent Baptist work in the growing, pioneer cattle town of Temuco. Miss Graham joined in the work of this devoted preacher and, together with other faithful and far-sighted missionaries whom the Board sent out, laid the foundation for what has proved to be an ever-enlarging Baptist work, which today has spread all over the republic.

A letter came in January, 1946, from Miss Graham's co-worker, Cornelia Brower, telling of the multitudes who came to the funeral to bear sorrowful tribute to the missionary they loved so dearly. Miss Graham died suddenly, away from home, and it was entirely fitting that her body should be taken back to Temuco to rest among the people she loved so devotedly and near the great school to which she had given her life. Miss Brower, the one of all others closest to Miss Graham, tells the story of the funeral:

> The funeral services were held at five in the afternoon. We moved her to our largest assembly hall, but that was not large enough to hold the people who came. Every one says it was the largest funeral ever held in Temuco. They estimated that there must have been two thousand people following the hearse on foot—students, ex-students, friends, official representatives, government high school teachers, and friends from all classes of society. It was more like a triumphal procession than a funeral.
>
> All the papers published something about her. At her grave there were several speeches made by representatives of different groups. The missionary group was represented by one of the Alliance missionaries; the graduates by one of her best-loved ex-students; the teachers by one of our faculty who loved and appreciated her; the government high school by the principal; the student body by one of the next year's high school boys; and the Chilean pastors by the pastor of the Baptist Church of Valdivia.

Agnes, greatheart for Christ in Chile! Hail and farewell! For you the night is past, and the dawn of an eternal day has come!

XII

Africa and India

THE EXECUTIVE SECRETARY of the Foreign Mission Board, beginning in June, 1934, had visited all the mission fields of Southern Baptists except Africa. Plans were made for the African visit in 1937, but a sudden outbreak of yellow fever made it necessary to postpone the visit until the following year. Accompanied by Mrs. J. B. Boatwright of South Carolina and Dr. and Mrs. M. T. Andrews of Texas, Mrs. Maddry and I sailed from New York on May 24. After spending ten days with our Italian Mission Board, we sailed from Liverpool on June 15 and landed at Lagos, West Africa, on June 30. A large delegation of missionaries and African men and women from the churches of Lagos and inland cities were at the dock to welcome us. The official welcome of the Baptists of the Lagos District was extended to our party in a public service in the spacious but crowded auditorium of the First Baptist Church. It was a colorful and inspiring sight. The singing was wonderful, and I could understand at once why the Negroes of the South are such gifted singers. Nigeria is the ancestral home of nearly all our black people of the South. I was hearing for the first time the black folk sing in their native tongue and in their original homeland. It was an experience never to be forgotten. The Boys' School in Lagos is one of the outstanding examples of missionary work in Nigeria.

We left Lagos on July 3 and made our first stop at Abeokuta. From the city as a center, we visited day by day the churches and schools of the Abeokuta District. Then for five weeks the tours continued from such centers as Iwo, Oyo, Shaki, Ogbomosho, Ibadan, Sapele, Benin City, and many other communities. Everywhere we went the welcome was generous and enthusiastic. I preached in churches and chapels, and when the crowds were too great to be accommodated in a house, I preached outdoors under the trees.

Nigeria takes its name from the Niger River (black) which is one of the great rivers of the world. Nigeria is one of the largest protectorates of the British Empire and is about the size of the combined area of Virginia, Alabama, Mississippi, North Carolina, South Carolina, Georgia, and Tennessee.

Nigeria is vastly rich in raw materials such as rubber, timber, cocoa, peanuts, palm kernels, palm oil, and tin ore. The leading occupation of the people is agriculture. The methods of farming are very primitive, but with modern machinery and advanced methods of cultivation, the yield from the soil would be almost limitless. The soil is exceedingly rich, and Nigeria is capable of feeding not only herself, but the British Isles also, if and when modern equipment and scientific methods of farming are put into practice.

It may be said without reservation that, except among those who have accepted Christianity, polygamy is practiced throughout Nigeria. It is the curse of the land. It is the ambition of most men to have as many wives as they can buy and to have many, many children. A man's social and political importance and his economic status are indicated by the number of wives he has been able to acquire and the number of children crowding his compound. His wives and children constitute his main source of wealth. It is considered, therefore, not a crime to be a polygamist, but rather a distinct honor. The women themselves, except Christians, approve of polygamy.

The twin evil of polygamy is easy and frequent divorce. The wife has no voice in the choice of her husband and she is often sadly disappointed by his brutality and ill-treatment. He cannot divorce her, but she can divorce him by simply paying back the dowry money paid her parents by the husband. There is always a surplus of unmarried men, and wives are at a premium. There are few unattached women in Nigeria. The divorced woman is always able to find another man who is willing to pay the dowry money and take her.

When we were in the capital city of all the Yorubas, the king came to hear me preach. It was the first gospel sermon he had ever heard. It is said that he had five hundred wives. Two of his favorite wives came with him to church.

I was greatly pleased at the progress of our work in the eighty-six years since T. J. Bowen of Georgia began his work as the first missionary. Today we have about 150 missionaries in Nigeria including some twelve American medical missionaries. There are 250 elementary schools, six high schools, five normal schools, one training school, and one theological seminary.

In Nigeria we have 283 churches, and in the Gold Coast there are 38 more. In 1953, there were 3,370 baptisms reported. We have four hospitals, five dispensaries, and in 1952 we treated a total of 38,912 patients. There was in 1952 a leper colony at Ogbomosho with 785 patients; also, there were several smaller settlements, and many lepers are being healed if they are treated in the early stages of the disease. Many patients are being treated with the new sulfone drugs. There is a Baptist church with a large membership in the Ogbomosho leper colony. The schools and hospitals in Nigeria are great evangelizing agencies.

In Oyo, Nigeria, at breakfast in the home of one of our missionaries, we were sitting beside Dr. George Green, when one of the table boys came and told the doctor that there was someone in the back yard of the Mission house waiting to see him. Dr. Green excused himself and went out. I thought that it was just one more case of sickness or suffering calling for the professional services of the doctor. Presently he returned smiling and, in answer to our inquiry for the reason of the joy that was written in his face, said that an old friend had come to call upon him and had brought him a calabash of green corn. I at once sensed a good story and induced the modest medical man to tell us the reason for the warm gratitude of the old man.

Several years ago, an old blind man had found his way to Dr. Green's clinic at Ogbomosho and had appealed to the doctor to give him back his eyesight. The doctor had examined him and found that he had been totally blind from cataracts for several years. Dr. Green performed the delicate operation. After several days of anxious waiting, the bandages were removed, and, to the amazement of the old man and the joy of the doctor, the patient could see. Dr. Green fitted him with glasses, and after a few weeks, when he was dismissed from the hospital, he had almost perfect eyesight.

The joy and gratitude of the old man knew no bounds. And the best part of the story is that during these days of waiting in the hospital, the medical missionary had taught him the love and mercy of a Saviour who was waiting to save him. The old man had found in the mission hospital something greater than his physical eyesight; he had found the glorious light of the Saviour's face in the pardon and forgiveness of his sins.

He went home and was gone for some days. Then one day he came back leading a string of ten blind men. Dr. Green examined them and saw that some were stone blind, while others were suffering from cataracts or other curable diseases of the eyes. The doctor took them in and operated on several of them. He was able to relieve some of them and give back their eyesight. Finally, the day came when he had to announce to those who were hopelessly blind that he could do nothing for them. Dr. Green said it was a heartbreaking hour that he would never forget. The blind men cried, wailed, and begged the missionary not to send them away in darkness but to give them back their eyesight, as he had the others. He tried to explain that he could not help them, but they thought that he was offended with them in some way and, therefore, would do nothing for them. They crawled over the floor, kissed the doctor's shoes, hugged his legs, and over and over in piteous appeal said: "Master, why are you angry? What have we done to offend you? Please give us back our eyesight, too."

Dr. Green said that whenever he visited Oyo, thereafter, the once blind man always came to him bringing his simple gifts as an expression of some of the gratitude in his heart for what the missionary doctor had done for him.

I shall never forget an African king who, after seeing some of our mission activities, begged us to send some missionaries to his people. It was several years before a couple was appointed to that field. In the meantime the old king died, and one of his last words was an inquiry when missionaries would be sent to his people.

Before I turn away from Africa, let me tell the story of the J. C. Powells, typical of the experiences of other missionaries.

In the days when our Board was crushed by debt and we had borrowed already too much at the banks, the Board said to these devoted missionaries, "You can't go back to Africa. We accept your resignation." They were down in North Carolina living with Mrs. Powell's widowed mother. I had just come to the Board as Executive Secretary and was trying to carry out the instructions of the Board. In a letter to Mr. and Mrs. Powell I said, "You cannot go back to Africa. We do not have the money for your expenses or salary. We are accepting your resignation. You will have to find other work." I had a letter from Mr. Powell in which he said, "We got the call to go to Africa from God. It is his plan for us to be out there with the black people. Now, the Board may say we cannot go, but God called us, and we will go."

I tried by correspondence to convince them they could not go, but failed. One cold, snowy Saturday I got on the train and went down to eastern North Carolina and spent Sunday with Mr. and Mrs. Powell. I tried to convince them they could not go back to Africa. They just smiled and said, "God called us to Africa, and he is going to send us back. We have been talking to him about this in prayer."

Mrs. Powell said, "Why, I have absolute faith that God will provide a way for us to go back when our furlough is over. I am busy sewing and getting our outfit together and packing our trunks."

Monday morning Mr. Powell took me to the train. The last thing I said was, "Now, just forget it, you can't go back to Africa."

He laughed and said, "Will you just do one thing for me—make reservation for us?"

I said, "I'll do that, but you cannot go."

He said, "Anyway, you make the reservation and get our passage. We will go back to Africa."

In a few days a letter came from Texas, signed by a woman of whom I never heard. She said, in substance, "I am a widow, a seamstress. I make my living by sewing. I have a girl who will be ready for college next fall. I have dreamed for years of sending her to college, and I have been praying to God to call her to be a missionary. I have saved up $150 toward the expenses for Lucille's college course. I saw in *Home and Foreign Fields* that Mr. and Mrs. Powell could not go back to Africa because there was no money provided. So Lucille and I prayed and decided to give the $150 to help send the Powells back. I am enclosing my check for $150."

I kept the check two or three days and sent it back with a note saying that the check wouldn't begin to pay for tickets for the Powells. They would cost $800, and their salary would be $1600. It was too much of a sacrifice to take the check for $150 which had been saved for Lucille's college course. The letter had hardly had time to get to Texas before the check came back again with a letter from the lady saying that God had told her to send the check, and I was to use it as far as it would go. The amazing thing that happened was the way money came in. One woman sent $800, another $50, another $100, and $500, and $800. The checks came from all over the South without anybody asking for them. Each one who sent money said God had told them to send it so the Powells could go back to Africa. The Powells came through Richmond on their way to Africa. We sat in my office and counted the money. There was enough left over to send back $500 to a woman in South Carolina.

World Missionary Conference in India

The World Missionary Conference met in Madras, India, during the last ten days of 1938, shortly after our visit to Africa. The Executive Secretary of the Foreign Mission Board of the Southern Baptist Convention was elected to represent the Baptists of the South in this significant and momentous conference. I left New York on the *Queen Mary* the middle of November and landed at Cherbourg, France. I went to Paris for a few days' conference with our European Secretary, Dr. Everett Gill. Dr. J. H. Rushbrooke, president, and Dr. W. O. Lewis, American secretary of the Baptist World Alliance, came to Paris for a conference concerning the forthcoming meeting of the Alliance in Atlanta. We spent Thanksgiving Day together, and early next morning I left by train for Marseilles. It was a tedious trip, and I was very tired when I reached this southern port of France and went aboard an English liner bound for Bombay, India.

I had seen China with her millions without Christ. I had seen Africa, in her superstition and heathenism, but words fail me when I try to tell of the poverty, superstition, degradation, and appalling sin of India. I was especially moved over the almost hopeless state of the untouchables in their isolation and economic misery. There were more than 60,000,000 untouchables in India. They were not allowed to associate in any way with the superior upper classes but were kept in poverty, crowded in the slums, separate and apart from their fellows. They were not permitted to drink at the public fountains or attend the public schools or play in the public parks. Only the lowest and most degraded forms of employment were open to them, such as common scavengers and cleaners of the open sewers. For one of the upper class to touch one of these hopeless ones was strictly forbidden. Truly their social and economic status was appalling beyond description. The sacred cows wandered through the streets, grazed on the public squares, and were held in far higher esteem than the untouchables. However, in recent years progress is being made in elevating the status of these people.

On my way to the Madras Missionary Conference I remained for some five days in Bombay along with the Methodist leaders from America. I was graciously entertained in the Methodist Mission House. Here I met Dr. Ambedkar, the leader of India's sixty million untouchables. The lady superintendent of the Methodist work in the Bombay area had assisted Dr. Ambedkar in editing and publishing his latest book. He was a brilliant scholar, and after finishing his undergraduate work in the Methodist University of Bombay, he came to America and took a doctor's degree from Columbia University. This Methodist superintendent was much concerned for the conversion of this great leader of India's untouchables. She gave a dinner for the American visitors, and Dr. Ambedkar was present. The missionary wanted him to come in contact with some of the religious leaders of America. The treatment accorded this leader of the untouchables by the religious fanatics of America, especially in some of his travels in the South, had given him a bad opinion of Christianity in America. To our question as to his attitude toward Christ, this brilliant leader of his people replied that he accepted Christ as a great teacher and friend of the lowly, but because of what he had seen of America's attitude toward the colored races, he could not accept him as Saviour. He kept referring to America as "Christian America." I tried to convince him that not all America was Christian, but he seemed to be obsessed with the idea that America was a Christian nation and was unjust in her treatment of all colored peoples.

It took a day and a night to cross India by train. The sleeping cars were just leather-covered couches, and every passenger had to provide his own sheets and blankets. Compared with an American Pullman car, the accommodations were anything but desirable. The World Missionary Conference met at one of the finest Christian mission colleges of India. The students were absent for the Christmas holidays, and all the facilities of the college were turned over to delegates attending the conference. The rooms were comfortable, and the campus and surroundings were attractive in every way. The college at Tambaram was fifteen miles from the great city of Madras, and there were trains to and from the city every hour.

The so-called "younger churches" from India, Africa, China, Japan, Burma, Thailand, Indonesia, and Europe sent large delegations. It was truly a brilliant and notable gathering. It was claimed that like Pentecost they were there from all over the world speaking many dialects and tongues. Surely God was in the meeting. It was an inspiring event when the roll call of the nations took place.

One of my most vivid impressions was that the leaders in the national churches were becoming the leaders of the Christian movement in their own lands and in the world.

The World Missionary Conference was organized along the most modern and efficient lines. Every member was assigned to work with some committee on "Findings." Dr. John R. Mott was chairman over all, and he appointed a chairman over each committee. We were given about ten days to complete our work and then plenary sessions were held at the close of the meetings to pass upon the findings of each group.

In the group meetings we soon found that no place was provided for new subjects not included in the printed agenda handed to the committees, and that we were supposed to approve the matters handed down to us by the guiding minds of the Conference.

Just at this time Southern Baptists were suffering persecution in Rumania at the hands of the Greek Orthodox Church. I thought that the Conference offered a splendid platform for the airing of this matter before all the world. Therefore, I introduced a resolution condemning this persecution and placing the Conference on record as opposed to the current outbreak. In the committee I was supported by Northern Baptists, Southern Methodists, and Presbyterians. All the delegates from state-controlled churches voted against us. I expected this and prepared to carry the matter to the plenary session of the Conference.

On the last night of the Conference our report of "findings" came up for adoption. There were beautiful speeches lauding the committee for such a statesmanlike report, and Dr. Mott asked if there was anyone else who desired to speak on the matter. I had sent up a note beforehand asking the right to be heard for ten minutes. The request was granted, and I went to the platform and stated my case. It gave me the chance to get before the whole Conference the fact that while we were there passing platitudes about church union and the beautiful example of almost universal co-operation, there were members of the Conference from Rumania persecuting their fellow Christians called Baptists and filling Rumanian jails with Baptist preachers. Our protest was rejected, as we expected, but delegates from all over the world, while not voting with us, came offering congratulations for the stand we had taken. Of course, the brethren from the countries where the churches are dominated by the state were displeased. They felt that it was unfortunate that the lovely harmony of the closing session of the Conference had been broken by the introduction of such a disturbing matter.

On Christmas Sunday, 1938, the American delegates to the World Missionary Conference were invited to spend the day with the American Baptist Mission in Madras. We worshiped with a large church made up entirely of untouchables. The pastor was an untouchable, highly educated and on fire with zeal for the lost. It was a never-to-be-forgotten hour. The singing was inspiring and uplifting. The sermon was delivered with great earnestness and enthusiasm. I saw the people all around us weeping, and they seemed profoundly moved. I, too, found myself moved with the people about me. Though I could not understand a word the preacher said, I knew it was an effective and Spirit-filled message.

We dined with the Northern Baptist missionaries, and, commenting on the sermon, I inquired as to the subject under discussion. One missionary friend replied that the pastor was preaching on the cross. In India I was seeing, first hand, after nearly a century and a half, some of the glorious results of the work of William Carey, the cobbler, and the Kettering Movement.

I went to sleep that night with a song of joy and thanksgiving in my heart over the outcome of that meeting at Kettering in 1792, when "thirteen nobodies" organized the first Baptist Foreign Missionary Society in the world and gave £ 13, 2 s, 6 d, about $63.00, to send the gospel to India's millions.

I sailed from Bombay on January 5, 1939. The weather was stormy, and the sea was rough. It was indeed a lonely and tiresome trip of three weeks. I had been planning for several years to write a new mission study book on Nigeria. Before going to Africa I had gathered a great deal of material concerning our Nigerian Mission, especially informing myself on the historic background. I knew the facts concerning the work and location of every missionary who had served during the many years of the life of the Mission. On the visit to Africa in the summer of 1938, I had tried to fit the historic data I had gathered into the work of every missionary who had served in Nigeria. While it was all fresh in my mind, I decided to write the book. On the three weeks' trip from Bombay to New York, I spent seven hours a day writing. It was an exhausting task, but when I reached New York, the first draft of the book was finished. It was published in the summer of 1939, under the title of *Day Dawn in Yoruba Land.* The book passed through several editions and had a wide sale among Southern Baptists. I reached home on the first of February tired but happy in the belief that the trip had been of some value to our foreign mission work and that God's blessing had been poured out upon us.

XIII

America's Day of Infamy

SUDDENLY there was a tremendous roar and the whole island seemed to shiver and surge like a mighty ship in the grip of a raging storm.

"There must be a terrible storm coming up. I do not think I ever heard such a crash of thunder. Do you have many such violent thunderstorms in Honolulu in mid-winter?"

"No," said the Japanese maid who was cleaning my room in the hotel. "It does not sound like thunder to me. It sounds more like bursting bombs and big guns. The whole earth seems to shake."

My window looked out toward Pearl Harbor. I pulled up the shade and to my amazement saw up amid the clouds a fighter plane, apparently out of control, partially enveloped in smoke. It was rolling and surging like an angry, billowing cloud. Some distance below the rolling plane, to the left, I saw a rapidly decending parachute. The cords were plainly visible but the pilot was hidden in boiling clouds of black smoke. The parachute seemed to have been caught in a terrible cross-fire of bursting shells.

The crashing roll of what I thought at first was thunder seemed to die away in a series of terrific explosions in the direction of the Pearl Harbor area.

There was a brief pause and a lull that was ominous of impending disaster. Then the roar of an anti-aircraft gun rent the stillness. This was followed by another and then a second terrific explosion that seemed to shake the city and surrounding hills to their very foundations.

It finally dawned on me that this was far more serious than a Sunday morning "alert" or a practice display of military and naval might.

I had reached Honolulu early Wednesday morning, December 3, 1941. The fifteen missionaries constituting the Hawaiian Baptist Mission were at the dock to give me a heart-warming and enthusiastic welcome. A committee of three from the Mission had been appointed to conduct me on an extensive survey of our work throughout Oahu, the island upon which Honolulu is situated. This first day we drove one hundred miles over the splendid boulevard which the American government has built around the perimeter of this main island of the Hawaiian group.

After visiting many villages and community centers of the sugar-cane and pineapple industry, about 4 o'clock we came to the winding stretch of road as it skips and skirts the red volcanic peaks surrounding Pearl Harbor. Suddenly as we rounded an out-jutting peak there burst into view the mighty American fleet riding peacefully at anchor on the placid, inland lake known as Pearl Harbor. It was without doubt the most imposing and impressive sight my eyes had ever looked upon.

"Look, boys, at that gigantic structure of the *Arizona.* It seems to me that one big bomb or shell rightly placed in that complicated and elaborate maze of steel would put the mighty ship out of control immediately."

"No," said a Texas missionary, with pride and enthusiasm, "that is the strongest battle fleet ever assembled at one anchorage. That fleet can whip any navy in the world."

With a sense of pride and confidence in the might of the American Navy to guard and defend our shores, we drove on into the city of Honolulu with a feeling of smug satisfaction that the Texas brother had expressed the sentiment of each of us.

It was a quiet, peaceful Sunday morning in semi-tropical Honolulu, at the crossroads of the Pacific. Fleecy clouds of vapor in lazy spirals floated around the summits of the red-tinted peaks of volcanic rock. The valleys were still shrouded in mists.

Far out to the west, with an occasional break in the clouds, one could see for a moment the majestic swell of the Pacific as it broke in long sweeps on the beach of the island of Oahu. The sweet and pungent odor of myriads of semi-tropical flowers filled the air. All nature seemed at rest, and the birds were singing with joy and abandon.

I was up early getting ready for three services to be held at different stations. I was to lay the cornerstone of a new church that day, and for Sunday night a meeting for the soldiers and sailors at Wheeler Field had been arranged. But the three sermons prepared for that day were not delivered.

Charles E. Maddry at seventy-six

Charles E. Maddry at the desk
used by Matthew T. Yates

Mrs. Charles E. Maddry in 1933

The clock in the bell tower of the University of Hawaii struck seven-forty-five. An eternity of agony crowded into ten minutes! Seven-fifty-five, and America's "day of infamy" would be ushered in!

After hearing the explosions I hastily made my way down the two flights of steps leading to the hotel lobby. At the foot of the stairs, I met the hotel manager. He was wringing his hands in an agony of hysteria, and calling out in a voice choking with sobs. "Vacate your rooms at once. Come down to the ground floor. The hotel may be struck any minute. It's the real thing. It's the real thing."

"What do you mean? *What* is the *real* thing?"

"It's war. It's war. The whole island is under attack of enemy bombers. It has just come in over the radio. We are at war."

"No, no, it surely can't be war!"

"Yes, it's war. The radio has just announced that the fleet at Pearl Harbor is under attack. Some of our ships have already been sunk. An enemy plane has been shot down with the emblem of the Rising Sun on the wings."

I ran toward the lobby, and it seemed to me that every guest in the hotel was already there or on the way. Many were in a wild panic of fear and hysteria. Children were crying, and there was fear and terrible confusion on every hand.

The radio was turned on full volume. It was blaring forth the details of the awful tragedy that was unfolding minute by minute. The most appalling and destructive war of all the ages had begun!

Many of the guests of the hotel were the wives and children of Army and Navy officers located at Pearl Harbor or at one of the airfields surrounding and guarding the naval base. These people were crowded about the radio, listening to the detailed account of the terrible tragedy in which their loved ones at that very moment were involved. The cries and sobs of the women and children were mingled in heart-rending confusion with the roar of bursting bombs as they fell in a crazy-quilt pattern over the stricken and helpless city. The answering chatter of antiaircraft guns, interspersed with the thunderous roar of great coastal defense guns, was maddening to nerves and emotions already strained to the breaking point.

Fires were raging all over the city, and there was continuous clanging of fire trucks trying to answer the calls from scattered areas.

For hours we kept close to the radio and heard a running description of the terrible catastrophe in which the destiny of our country was so vitally involved.

Sandwiched in between the story of the sudden and murderous attack upon our naval base and protecting airfields were the orders and instructions of both the civil and military authorities for the conduct and guidance of the frightened and bewildered populace of the stricken city.

"Everyone must get off the streets at once. Stay under cover. Bombs are falling in all parts of the city. Many civilians have already been wounded, and a number have been killed."

"All cars must get off the streets and stay off. Run them onto lawns and parks. Stay off the streets! This means everybody! We are not asking you! We are telling you! All civilians are ordered off the streets until further notice."

"Governor Poindexter has ordered a state of emergency for the entire territory."

"A bomb has just fallen on the grounds of the Governor's palace. Governor Poindexter was in his office but was uninjured."

"Fifty enemy planes have been counted over Pearl Harbor. The Rising Sun emblem was plainly visible on the wing tips."

"Wave after wave of Japanese bombers are streaming through the clouded morning sky from the southwest. Each plane seems to know its assigned target. Their aim is deadly accurate and the results are destructive and appalling."

The first extra edition of the *Advertiser,* the morning newspaper, was out at 10:30 a.m. There was a mad scramble for copies, and the supply was sold out before the newsboy reached the hotel lobby. Here follow some of the headlines in bold type:

"Emergency hospital announces a list of six killed and twenty-one wounded."

"Fort Shafter announces that the entire Island of Oahu is under sporadic attack."

"City in uproar ten minutes after attack begins."

"First indication of surprise raid came shortly before eight o'clock when antiaircraft guns around Pearl Harbor began sending up a thunderous barrage."

"Just three minutes after the attack was begun, the first American gun was fired by a young naval recruit. Acting on his own responsibility, he manned a machine gun and it was reported that his firing was deadly effective."

"A vast cloud of black smoke arose from the naval base, and from Hickham Field where raging flames could be seen."

"Oil tank of city set afire."

"Huge fires were raging at Pearl Harbor at 1:10 p.m. Five vessels appeared to have been destroyed in the several air raids. One ship has turned over on its side. Fires raging in four others seemed to be gaining in intensity as they settled in the water."

"A dispatch intercepted from Imperial Headquarters in Tokyo says Japan entered state of war with U.S. and Great Britain in Western Pacific since dawn today."

"Part of fleet that has escaped is moving out to sea."

The attack began with wave after wave of Japanese bombers diving out of the clouds upon Pearl Harbor, Hickham Field, Schofield Barracks, and Ford Island, where many of the families of naval officials lived.

The enemy planes came over in successive waves nearly all day and into the night. The first attack, which came at 7:55 a.m., lasted nearly an hour. The second wave came at 9:15, the third at 11:39, and the fourth at 11:49. There was a lull for a while, then another attack came at 7:15 p.m., and the last at 9:15 that night.

I was looking out of my room window at the awesome fires rolling up from the burning battleship, *Arizona*, whose magazine had exploded. Secretary Knox has described the awful tragedy of sailors swimming through burning oil. I heard the dreadful whine of a bomb coming at an oblique angle. It seemed an eternity of agony before it passed the end of the hotel, the length of two windows from my room. It landed in the school grounds adjoining the hotel and left an excavation big enough for a court house! Someone asked me later how *long* I heard the whine of this coming bomb. I replied that it *seemed* like about thirty days!

It is now known that many of the Japanese aviators who wrought such havoc in Honolulu were educated in the high schools and the University of Honolulu. They knew everything about the islands—the defenses and vital areas. They knew, for instance, where the officers and top sergeants slept in the barracks. They knew where every ship was berthed and where every power plant was located. They knew how many ships were in the harbor for the week ends, their names, and where they were anchored. At least two submarines followed the last warship in through the mine fields on Saturday night.

There is ample evidence that those Japanese bombers were "suicide squads." They were bent on doing all the damage they possibly could, and for them the loss of life was only incidental.

A suicide bomber crashed within fifteen feet of the sub-station of the Hawaiian Electric Power Company that fed Wheeler Field. Two homes were wrecked and burned as the plane dived for the power station. The bodies of the two Japanese airmen were horribly burned. One of our missionaries saw the small metal tablet taken off the burned Japanese bomber. On that bit of metal was the inscription: "Bendix Airplane Corporation, New Jersey, U. S. A." The wings of the plane were made of tin, but it was powered by an American engine, driven by American aviation gasoline, and its bombs of destruction were made of American scrap iron.

Another suicide bomber dived for the broad doorway of the repair shop at Wheeler Field. The work benches were crowded with workmen. The enemy bomber wrought a fearful havoc of death and destruction before it came to rest half-way through the long workshops.

Bombers made repeated death dives upon the decks of American battleships. Japanese airmen seemed utterly indifferent to death, if only they achieved the objective set for them.

By ten o'clock on Sunday the refugees from all the airfields and naval and military areas had begun their tragic flight into the city. The public school buildings, hotels, churches, and private homes were soon crowded. Many mothers had fled with their little children without even a change of clothing. I had read of the horror of seeing refugees fleeing from burning homes and murderous war. Now I had witnessed it all.

In the first group of refugees to reach my hotel in mad flight was a young mother, the wife of a naval officer whose ship had gone down. With her were the three little children. The mother was in the terrible grip of hysterical fear, and the little children, clad only in their pajamas, were sobbing with exhaustion and fright. I was glad for a few minutes to get away from the blare of the terrible radio and give what assistance I could. They were taken in and given a room. Friends crowded around with love and sympathy to comfort the stricken and distressed group.

This case was typical, and it was the beginning of the confused and disorganized flight of refugees from Ford Island (the island in the center of Pearl Harbor where Navy personnel and families lived), and from the areas of the surrounding airfields. The number of refugees increased as that tragic Sunday dragged its weary way on toward noon. The murderous attack had been in progress for four hours, and the lists of Army and Navy dead and wounded were increasing every minute as the successive waves of Japanese bombers came over, dropped their loads of death and went back to their mother ships for more. Some of those who fled into the city had heard the worst already concerning husband or father. Others were paralyzed with the fearful dread that any minute might become a reality as the radio continued to unfold the story of the unspeakable tragedy that was being inflicted on America's first line of defense just over the peaks behind Devil's Head.

Over the radio all day, from 9 a.m. until midnight, there came these entries often repeated. One plea was for blood donors. "Need desperate. Report at once to Queen's Hospital." The reason for this urgent entreaty so often repeated throughout the day was apparent to everyone when the long lists of wounded and mangled soldiers and sailors came in during the days that followed.

Another plea that brought a pang of fear and dread to every heart was the continuous call for doctors and nurses. Finally, the names of more than forty city doctors were read, and they were requested to report at once to the several hospitals. The plea for nurses was equally insistent. I knew by these appeals that the casualty lists were large and increasing with fearful rapidity.

Another plea that was tragically revealing was for ambulances. When the supply was exhausted there came the entreaty, repeated over and over by the hour, for trucks for the transportation of the wounded to the various hospitals. "Ambulances needed desperately. Every available truck report to authorities at Pearl Harbor. Already 100 trucks have answered call for ambulance duty. Many more needed at once."

There came also this plea from Hickham Field where the destruction and loss of life had been so heavy: "Hickham Field appeals for emergency water supply for domestic purposes." Early Sunday afternoon there came this gratifying announcement: "F. H. Davies and Company furnished a fleet of one hundred trucks for Hickham Field."

We know now that the Japanese had planned weeks ahead every minute detail of the proposed surprise attack. To make certain that all suspicion might be allayed, they had sent a special peace delegation to Washington. Their hypocritical envoys kept up their pretense for a peaceful solution of the differences existing between the two nations until the actual attack was in progress. We know now that the orders had gone forth for the sailing of the convoy of death at the very time the special peace envoys were on their way by airplane to Washington. The task force, under sealed orders, sailed from a port in northern Japan about ten days before the date agreed upon for the attack. The enemy force followed the Great Northern Circle route until, just off the Aleutian Islands, they turned due south for some seven hundred miles to their appointed rendezvous. Five hundred miles off Honolulu to the southwest, the squadron met the submarine flotilla that had been dispatched to the Western Pacific some weeks ahead.

After opening their sealed orders, the commanders rehearsed in detail the attack planned for dawn the next morning. At dusk on Saturday afternoon the fleet sailed with leisurely confidence toward the unsuspecting naval base at Pearl Harbor. At the first sign of day, the death squadron came to a halt three hundred miles southwest of Honolulu. In the murky dawn of a quiet and peaceful Sunday morning, fifty-odd planes, weighted with their terrible missiles of death, took off for Pearl Harbor.

The timing was perfect. In blissful ignorance of the impending danger, the Army and Navy personnel were taking things quietly after two weeks at sea. Saturday had been a payday. Discipline had been relaxed. Gay parties for both officers and men had helped to while away the fleeting hours of Saturday night. Why worry? The great ships were riding quietly and serenely at their berths. Everybody was taking it easy and sleeping late!

Moreover, the quarter of a million inhabitants of the beautiful, gay, and irresponsible city of Honolulu were sleeping after a night of revelry, feasting, and dancing. Why restraint? The fleet was in, payday on Saturday had quickened the flow of mirth.

For some two weeks the Army and Navy personnel had been under "alert," but only for local sabotage. There was no fear or expectation of danger from without. There were 70,000 Japanese nationals in the city of Honolulu. Not knowing who were loyal or disloyal, it was deemed the part of wisdom to watch for local sabotage. All planes on the several airfields around the naval base for the week end had been parked close together so that there could be efficient watch against incendiary fires. Also, as an extra precaution, all gasoline and guns were removed from bombers and fighting planes. In fact, the investigation brought out the fact that many of the fighters and practice planes had never been supplied with weapons of any kind except dummies.

It has since been revealed that there was no systematic patrol of the Hawaiian off-shore, and radar apparatus was left unmanned. A recruit, ambitious to learn all he could about radar technique, tuned in less than an hour before the attack and detected the approach of a large detachment of unidentified planes. He reported the matter to his superior and was told to sign off as it was doubtless a squadron of American planes on reconnaissance.

The tragedy of Sunday, December 7, 1941, will go down in history as the most humiliating, shameful, and unnecessary disaster that has ever befallen us as a nation. Thirty-three hundred sailors and soldiers, the vast majority of them under twenty-one years of age, were suddenly hurled into eternity, without a moment's warning. Eight hundred others were wounded, some of them horribly mangled. The long lists of civilians who perished—many of them little children—crowded the columns of the daily papers until one was sick at heart over it all. There were mass funerals from Monday on through the week until Saturday noon. Four hundred were buried in Wheeler Field at one time. The heartbreak and sorrow of it will follow me as long as I live.

All day Sunday and through Sunday night I saw the flames from the burning *Arizona* leaping into the air. The enemy with fiendish accuracy dropped a bomb down her smokestack. Her magazine exploded, and the mighty ship blew up and sank. All of the other ships have been raised except the *Arizona.* Seven hundred of her gallant crew sleep at the bottom of Pearl Harbor. I saw the mass funeral of the remainder of the *Arizona's* men who were lost.

Sunday was a dreadful night spent in total darkness. We greatly feared there would be other attacks that night and the days following. We feared also that saboteurs would burn the city that night.

God grant that America shall never experience what I saw, and may he forgive America for her senseless and greedy policy of continuing, for four years, to sell oil, gasoline, scrap iron, and airplane engines to Japan for the destruction of helpless China and the death of untold millions of innocent men, women, and children. It had come back to us in fearful judgment!

XIV

Retirement from the Secretaryship

I FINISHED MY VISITS to all the mission fields of our Board with the trip to the newly-established Hawaiian Mission in December, 1941. I was tired when I went out to Honolulu. I came back home completely exhausted, nervous, and sleepless. The burden of the work in the homeland, the continuous travel in foreign lands, the effort to pay off the crushing debt on the Board, together with the heavy responsibility of the administration of the affairs of the Board at home and abroad, had undermined my health. I knew I was headed for a scrap heap unless some way was found for complete rest. This was impossible as long as I remained Executive Secretary.

After many weeks of earnest prayer for divine guidance, I presented the following to the Board at the October meeting in 1943:

Statement of the Executive Secretary

Eleven years ago the Foreign Mission Board in annual session called me to be Executive Secretary of the Foreign Board. Without going into details or attempting to recount the struggles of these years, I now come to request that the Foreign Mission Board at this semi-annual session appoint a committee of nine members, constituting one-fourth of the membership of the Board, to search out and recommend to the Board for election at the semi-annual meeting in April, 1944 an associate executive secretary who, with some months of training with the Executive Secretary, should be able to take over the work by the close of the year, 1944.

At the close of the year 1944 I will be within three months of my sixty-ninth birthday. This will complete twelve years of service with this Board as Executive Secretary, and this added to twelve years in the secretaryship in North Carolina will complete twenty-four years of hard laborous and exhausting work as a general denominational secretary.

The work of this Board in both Europe and China will have to be completely reorganized. It is a task that is going to require the boundless energy and strength of a younger man. This man, by all means, ought to be in training not later than the semi-annual meeting of the Board next October for this challenging and exacting task that lies ahead for Southern Baptists.

We firmly believe that every door in the world will be open for the entrance of the gospel when this terrible war comes to an end. You need a young man in this crucial and exacting position for your leader for the first quarter of a century of new Southern Baptists' foreign mission work that soon will be dawning for us. The time will be all too short to seek out and train such a man.

Please be assured of my deep and abounding gratitude for the boundless way in which you have supported me through these eleven crucial and epoch-making years it has been my privilege to serve with you. And be assured, further, that all of my strength and whatever ability God may give me will be at your disposal until the Lord shall call me unto himself.

The Board replied in the following statement:

IN APPRECIATION OF DR. CHARLES E. MADDRY

When, at his insistent request, Dr. Charles E. Maddry retires from the executive secretary-ship of the Foreign Mission Board of the Southern Baptist Convention, he can review with pardonable pride and satisfaction and with deep gratitude the tokens of favor, human and divine, which have attended, from the first day until now, his leadership.

Baptists have always believed, when they have sincererly sought it, in providential guidance in the selection of their leaders. That faith has had another signal confirmation in the call of Dr. Maddry to be our secretary. When he began his work in January 1933, neither we nor he fully realized how his background, training, and experience had unconsciously prepared him for the duties and difficulties of the most important and responsible post of service in our Southern Baptist Convention. But as perplexing problems and delicate situations developed requiring wisdom, understanding, patience, common sense, and religion we became thankfully aware of the resources he had accumulated in his previous manifold ministries. His pastorates, rural and urban, gave him the point of view of pastors and laymen and saved him from secretarial detachment, and from speaking down to people. His ambition for an education, and his training at college and seminary, his superintendency of education in his home county in North Carolina, and his connection as trustee of the University of his native State added an intellectual breadth and outlook which have served him well and the Board in formulating our educational policies both here and in other lands. His eleven years as General Secretary of the Board of Missions of North Carolina equipped him to deal intelligently with denominational activities, State and Southwide.

Thus to the major work of his career he brought physical strength, mental vigor, breadth of interest, and an utter devotion to the Cause he was to champion.

And all these qualities were needed in 1933 when we seemed to be at our wits' end. The shadow of a world-wide depression still enveloped us. There was unsettlement in the homeland and uncertainty about our missionary work abroad. Our well-nigh economic bankruptcy was reflected in our lowered morale and the courses of retreat. It took a stout heart to sound a note of hope.

It was here that our Secretary made to our Board and to Southern Baptists his most distinctive contribution. We humbly and gratefully recall the ascending road we traveled together during the past twelve years. The statistical figures on March 12, 1943 were still red, only they were crimsoned by the sacrifices of many loyal devoted people who were determined that our honor must be preserved and our work maintained and enlarged. Dr. Maddry in recounting our liberation from the bondage of debt has never failed to magnify the organizations and individuals that together made possible our recovery. But the fact remains that all these achievements rest back on and spring from spiritual factors and inspirations which no organizations, programs, techniques, and appeals could ever have produced. Faith in God, in the cause of Christianizing the world, faith in ourselves, and faith in our people we needed. We were apologetic, on the defensive, and suggestible to the counsels of despair. He imparted to us the contagion of his own faith, courage, vision, and hope. Our unpayable debt to Dr. Maddry is the new spirit he gave us. Our romantic statistics are the consequences of the confidence he inspired, the spiritual dynamic he possessed, and which his fellow-workers caught.

His twelve years as secretary was a period of expanding horizons for us and for him. His journeys to every Southern Baptist mission field yielded rich dividends for us and for the missionaries. His insight into the problems of preachers, teachers, nurses, and doctors working with race and in countries different from America, his comprehension of their perplexities today and their still greater ones in the adjustments that must be made after the War have been reflected in his plans and proposals for the next period of missionary work by Southern Baptists. Growing out of recognized needs has come *The Commission*, a magazine which is already beginning to realize the hope of the founder in giving Southern Baptists by pen and picture an intelligent understanding of the peoples of the world and our obligation to them. That the type of person who goes as missionary may be fitted by personality, background, culture, and ability to interpret appealingly our faith to the educated and the primitives, a personnel director gives his time to finding the ablest young men and women of our colleges. Notable among the advances in the last years has been the appointment of regional secretaries, and in every other department of our growing work administrative wisdom has been shown in meeting each new situation, in establishing new fields, and increasing the number of missionaries wherever doors have been open.

Noteworthy among the many achievements of this administration has been more than a million dollars given for the relief of the hungry in the famine-stricken areas of other lands.

Our missionary enterprise is the unifying center of Southern Baptists. Its appeal furnished momentum and lifting power for every other cause we support, and the Secretary of this Board has from the beginning in 1845 been the symbol and the incarnation of that work. Dr. Maddry satisfied that demand and fulfilled that expectation. He has been persuasive in our pulpits and on our platforms. With so large and divergent a constituency as compose the Southern Baptist Convention it is no easy task to keep them with one mind and purpose, and working together. Not the least of his achievements is that in every relationship he has sustained, with pastors, and laymen, with office staff, and missionaries he has won and kept their respect, their confidence, and their affection. And they and we think of him as a great Christian and so a great servant. Our Foreign Mission Board has been blessed of God in the men who have been our secretaries. Each faced problems springing out of the period in which he served. Each did his day's work, and faithfully. In that noble succession Dr. Maddry has walked. He has helped to make his predecessors' contributions secure. He has given security, stability to our own day, and has laid the foundation upon which his successors may build in confidence. We remember him as God's gift to us.

We are thankful that we are to continue to have—and we hope for many a day—his wisdom, his experience, and his great gifts at the service of our Board.

We would convey to Mrs. Maddry our grateful appreciation for the reinforcement, understanding, and sympathy she has given to our work, to the missionaries, and supremely to her husband.

We wish for them a long afternoon rich in the best blessings of God.

Solon B. Cousins
John L. Slaughter
W. R. Pettigrew
T. C. Ecton

At the June, 1944 meeting of the Board, the Board elected my successor as seen in the following news item published in the *Richmond Times-Dispatch:*

BAPTISTS ELECT DR. RANKIN MISSION BOARD SECRETARY

Dr. M. T. Rankin, former missionary to China, yesterday was elected by the Foreign Mission Board of the Southern Baptist Convention as executive secretary of the board. Dr. Rankin will assume office on Jan. 1, 1945, succeeding Dr. Charles E. Maddry, who desires to be relieved of the administrative duties of the office after having served for 12 years. By request of the Foreign Mission Board, Dr. Maddry will continue as field secretary through 1945, the centennial year of the board.

During Dr. Maddry's term of leadership as executive secretary, the board has liquidated its entire indebtedness, which, when he became secretary, amounted to $1,625,000. The work has been increased and the board now has 502 active missionaries in 17 foreign countries, while Southern Baptists have grown in membership from 4,000,000 to 5,500,000 during this period.

Dr. Rankin is a native of South Carolina, having been born at Newberry, S. C., July 28, 1894, the son of Rev. and Mrs. W. M. Rankin, Sr. He received his education at Wake Forest College, Furman University, and Southern Baptist Theological Seminary. He has the degrees of A. B. from Wake Forest, Th.M. and Ph.D. from Southern Baptist Seminary and received the honorary degree of Doctor of Divinity from Union Seminary in 1936 and William Jewell College in 1944. He was ordained by the First Baptist Church, Durham, N. C., in 1914, and was appointed to the Foreign Mission Board as a missionary to China, June 8, 1921. On March 8, 1922, he was married to Miss Valleria Greene, of North Carolina (born in China), daughter of Dr. and Mrs. G. W. Greene, for many years missionaries to China. Dr. and Mrs. Rankin have two daughters, Page, who recently graduated from Meredith College, and Mary Lee, who is in high school in Richmond.

While in China, Dr. Rankin served as professor and later as president of Graves Theological Seminary at Canton. In 1935 he was elected secretary for the Orient, which position he had held since that time. He was in Hong Kong when that city was captured by the Japanese and for several months he was interned by the Japanese in Stanley Camp. He came home on the Gripsholm on its first exchange trip in August, 1942.

For eight and one-half years Theron Rankin led Southern Baptists in a glorious fashion in their world mission advance. Then, on June 27, 1953, the tidings of his death from dread leukemia were flashed to his fellow workers in many lands. His last written missionary challenge closed with these words: "I am much more afraid of standing at the door of the new day of advance in the coming of God's kingdom and having God pass me by as he moves on, seeking those who will dare to follow him out into the world of this day. I would not dare to be left standing there."

On January 1, 1902, I began my ministry as pastor of the Baptist Church in Hillsboro, the county seat of Orange County. Hillsboro is an old town, laid out in 1753. As already indicated, it was at one time during colonial days the capital of the state. After winning the drawn battle of Guilford Court House, on March 15, 1781, Cornwallis retreated to Hillsboro and set up the royal standard, believing that the loyal Tories would flock to his standard and that he would then be able to overrun all the Province of North Carolina.

When I first became pastor of the Hillsboro Baptist Church in 1902, the congregation was without much financial strength. There were only twenty-one members. By 1952 the church had grown to a membership of something over two hundred members and was able to pay an adequate salary together with a comfortable parsonage.

I retired as Executive Secretary of the Foreign Mission Board in 1945. After a season of retirement, I had grown restless and "home sick" for the pastorate. When the church invited me to come as interim pastor, I accepted and came with the expectation of staying a few months. After almost three years I am still there. The congregation has increased, the financial contributions of the church have more than doubled, many new members have been baptized into the fellowship of the church, and a new day of hope and enthusiasm has come.

Because of the Civil War and the loss of the building fund, the church house was not finished until 1870. Through all the years the members felt sorely the need for Sunday school equipment. The matter was agitated at intervals but nothing had been done. At one time brick were purchased and placed on the grounds. The undertaking seemed so far beyond the ability of the congregation that the brick were disposed of and the task abandoned.

The church in the meantime took out Building and Loan stock, and when I came, there was the sum of fifteen thousand dollars accumulated toward the building of a Sunday school annex. We raised twenty thousand dollars more, and the long-dreamed of educational building was begun.

The church was organized on November 3, 1853, and in November, 1953, we celebrated its centennial. Our new building was completed, and it was a great occasion in the life of the church. The building is modern and up-to-date in every particular and will care for a graded Sunday school of five hundred pupils.

I have been preaching for fifty-three years and trust in the providence of God to complete the "circle" and finish my earthly ministry here where I began in 1901. Here in this dear little church I married Emma Parker on May 2, 1906.

The years have been good to us, and the Lord has richly blessed us. We have one daughter, Katharine, who has been everything to us that we could wish. She married Robert Watson Severance of South Carolina. They have three children, Katherine Maddry, Robert Watson II, and Sarah Watson.

I have now come to the end of the winding trail. The sun is long past the meridian; the shadows are slowly lengthening. Soon it will be sunset and darkness, but best of all, it will be sunrise in the morning!